D0007874

letters to a
young conservative

Also by Dinesh D'Souza

Illiberal Education:
The Politics of Race and Sex on Campus

The End of Racism:
Principles for a Multiracial Society

Ronald Reagan:
How an Ordinary Man Became an Extraordinary Leader

The Virture of Prosperity:
Finding Values in an Age of Techno-Affluence

What's So Great About America

Dinesh D'Souza

letters to a
young conservative

BASIC
BOOKS

A Member of the Perseus Books Group

Published by Basic Books,
A Member of the Perseus Books Group

Library of Congress Cataloging-in-Publication Data
 D'Souza, Dinesh, 1961-
   Letters to a young conservative / Dinesh D'Souza.
    pm. cm.— (The art of mentoring series)
  ISBN 0-465-01733-9 (hardcover)
   1. Conservatism—United States—Correspondence. 2. Youth—
United States—Political activity. 3. Politicians—United States—
Correspondence. 4. Right and left (Political science) I. Title. II.
Series
 JC573.2.U6 D76 2002
 320.52'0973—dc21

                                                    202008679

02 03 04 / 10 9 8 7 6 5 4 3 2 1

For Jeffrey Hart,
who showed me the world

Contents

Contents

1
Conservatives vs. Liberals

Dear Chris,

Thanks for your letter. I'm glad you enjoyed my talk at your university. Can you believe the number of protesters who showed up? There were people from the International Socialist group, the Spartacus League, the Coalition to Save Humanity, even some jobless guys from the local community. Wow, did they create a ruckus! Apparently they were distributing copies of a pamphlet called "Who Is Dinesh D'Souza?" I didn't see the pamphlet until later, but I discovered from it that I am a racist, a liar, a stooge of the ruling class, and an enemy of the people. All of which I hadn't realized until I read the pamphlet.

I don't know whether you are aware this, but the protesters almost prevented me from speaking. When I arrived, they had already surrounded the building. They were screaming into bullhorns and carrying placards that

read DINESH D'SOUZA: RACIST AGENT OF U.S. CAPITAL-
ISM AND IMPERIALISM. As I made my way through the
demonstrators, behind heavy security, I gave the protesters
the thumbs-up signal and told them, "Fight on, brothers
and sisters." This seemed to make them angrier. One of
them yelled, "You'll be lucky to get out of here alive!"

Despite the university's rule against bringing placards and bullhorns into the auditorium, the protesters
managed to force their way inside. I am sure you found
their gyrations on the stage quite a sight. My amusement
over their antics subsided, however, when they began to
disrupt my lecture with their shouts and chants. As you
saw, the dean of the college had to warn the demonstrators to hold their fire until the question period, or else
they would be evacuated. Only then did they quiet down
and allow me to speak.

Undoubtedly the high point of the evening occurred
near the end of my talk when the large, disheveled
woman came rolling up the aisle shouting, "We don't
need a debate! Stop this man from speaking!" My usual
strategy in such circumstances is to try to calm the pro-
tester down and engage in a discussion, but this time
there was no point. Finally, the woman was dragged
from the room by the campus police. On her way out
she yelled, "I am being censored! I am being censored!"

Yes, the American campus has become an interesting
place for a conservative. I cannot blame you for asking,
What has happened to liberalism? Where did it go
wrong? Is this what liberals stand for?

Today, alas, it is. But in saying this, I am not describing liberalism in its original or classical sense. We need to understand the big changes that have come over liberalism. The term *liberal*, in its Greek meaning, refers to the free man, as opposed to the slave. Liberals were originally the partisans of liberty. The American founders, for example, were committed to three types of freedom: economic freedom, political freedom, and freedom of speech and religion. In their classical liberal view, freedom meant limiting the power of government, thus increasing the scope for individual and private action. The spirit of this philosophy is clearly conveyed in the formulations of the Bill of Rights: "Congress shall make no law . . . "

This classical liberalism underwent two dramatic changes in the last century: the revolution of the 1930s, and the revolution of the 1960s. The revolution of the 1930s, the FDR revolution, was based on the assumption that rights are not meaningful unless we have the means to exercise them. As Franklin Roosevelt himself argued, people who lack life's necessities are *not free*. Roosevelt believed that to give citizens true liberty, the government should insure them against deprivation, against the loss of a job, against calamitous illness, and against an impoverished old age. Thus the liberal revolution of the 1930s introduced a new understanding of freedom that involved a vastly greater role for government than the American founders intended.

The second liberal revolution occurred in the 1960s. Its watchword was "liberation," and its great prophet was Jean-Jacques Rousseau. Before the sixties, most Americans believed in a universal moral order that is external to us, that makes demands on us. Our obligation was to conform to that moral order. Earlier generations, right up to the "greatest generation" of World War II, took for granted this moral order and its commandments: Work hard and try to better yourself, be faithful to your spouse, go when your country calls, and so on.

But, beginning in the sixties, several factions—the antiwar movement, the feminist movement, the gay activist movement, and so on—attacked that moral consensus as narrow and oppressive. They fought for a new ethic that would be based not on external authority but on the sovereignty of the inner self. This is the novel idea that received its most powerful expression in Rousseau's writing. To the American founders' list of freedoms, Rousseau added a new one: inner freedom, or moral freedom. Rousseau argues that we make major decisions—whom to love, what to become, what to believe—not by obeying our parents, teachers, preachers, or even God. Rather, we make such decisions by digging deep within ourselves and listening to the voice of nature. This is the idea of being "true to yourself." It is the new liberal morality.

Now that we have a sense of what liberals believe, let us contrast their views with those of the conservatives. Modern American conservatism is very different from European conservatism, or from conservatism traditionally understood. For one thing, conservatism in this country is "modern," and for another, it is "American." Ours is not the "throne and altar" conservatism that once defined European conservatism, and that is still characteristic of many Europeans on the right. These conservatives were true reactionaries. They sought to preserve the ancien régime and the prerogatives of king and church against the arrival of modern science, modern capitalism, and modern democracy.

American conservatives are different because America is a revolutionary nation. For the founders, the ancien régime was the world they had left behind in Europe. Ours is a country founded by a bunch of guys sitting around a table in Philadelphia and deciding to establish a "new order for the ages." Being a conservative in America means conserving the principles of the American revolution. (One of the most conservative groups in America calls itself the Daughters of the American Revolution.) Paradoxically, American conservatism seeks to conserve a certain kind of liberalism! It means fighting to uphold the classical liberalism of the founding from assault by liberalism of a different sort.

Classical liberalism, however, does not wholly define modern American conservatism. There is an added element: a concern with social and civic virtue. The term *virtue* has become a bad word in some quarters of American life. (It is especially unpopular with the chronically wicked and depraved.) Young people, especially, tend to associate it with finger-wagging and with people who tell you how to live your life. This is a very narrow view of virtue: It applies only to what it is good to do, rather than what it is good to be and what it is good to love.

The conservative virtues are many: civility, patriotism, national unity, a sense of local community, an attachment to family, and a belief in merit, in just desserts, and in personal responsibility for one's actions. For many conservatives, the idea of virtue cannot be separated from the idea of God. But it is not necessary to believe in God to be a conservative. What unifies the vast majority of conservatives is the belief that there are moral standards in the universe and that living up to them is the best way to have a full and happy life.

Conservatives recognize, of course, that people frequently fall short of these standards. In their personal conduct, conservatives do not claim to be better than anyone else. Newt Gingrich was carrying on an affair at the same time that Bill Clinton was romancing Monica Lewinsky. But for conservatives, these lapses do not provide an excuse to get rid of the standards. Even hypocrisy—professing one thing but doing another—is in the conservative view preferable to a denial of standards because such denial leads to moral chaos or nihilism.

Since modern conservatism is dedicated both to classical liberalism and to virtue, it is open to the charge of contradiction. What happens when there is a tension between liberty and virtue? Conservatives are often accused of resolving the tension by opting for liberty in the economic domain, but for virtue in the social domain. If liberals inconsistently hold that government should get out of the bedroom and into the pocketbook, conservatives appear to espouse the opposite philosophy of government: "Out of the pocketbook and into the bedroom."

Conservatives find this slogan amusing, but only because of its absurdity. I certainly don't know of any conservative who has advocated government surveillance in a person's bedroom. But it is true that the conservatives are willing at times to curtail liberty. When there is a threat to national security, as in the aftermath of the September 11 terrorist attacks, conservatives believe that to protect citizens' lives it may be necessary to curtail certain freedoms. Conservatives in general see nothing wrong with restricting pornography, with limiting the legal benefits of marriage to heterosexual couples, or with outlawing the use of hard drugs.

Thus neither conservatives nor liberals are the unqualified partisans of freedom. Both groups believe in a certain *kind* of freedom. What really distinguishes conservatives from liberals is not that one is for freedom and the other is against freedom; rather, what separates them is that they have different substantive views of what constitutes the good life.

Let us make a list of the liberal virtues: equality, compassion, pluralism, diversity, social justice, peace, autonomy, tolerance. Liberals become impassioned when they use these terms: They make up the moral priorities of the modern liberal worldview. By contrast, conservatives emphasize other virtues: merit, patriotism, prosperity, national unity, social order, morality, responsibility. Both sides are willing to place occasional restraints on freedom to achieve their substantive vision of the good society. Indeed, some liberals attach little importance to freedom. The Columbia radicals felt perfectly justified in trying to silence my talk: In their view, I have forfeited my right to free speech because I oppose their leftist agenda.

There is some overlap in the moral vocabulary that liberals and conservatives use. Both speak of "equality," although they mean different things by the term. Conservatives emphasize the equality of *rights*, and they are quite willing to endure inequalities that are the product of differential capacity or merit. Liberals emphasize the equality of *outcomes*, and they tend to attribute inequality to the unequal opportunities that have been provided by society. Another term that both liberals and conservatives use is "morality," but conservatives tend to define morality personally, while liberals define it socially. Conservatives find it hard to believe that a sexual reprobate can be a good person, but many liberals who acknowledge Bill Clinton's personal failings nevertheless consider him an admirable fellow because of his public positions in favor of the poor and women's rights.

Since conservatives and liberals have different conceptions of the good society, their priorities are different, and this leads to contrasting policy positions. Conservatives emphasize economic growth, while liberals emphasize economic redistribution. Conservatives like to proclaim their love of country, while liberals like to proclaim their love of humanity. Conservatives insist that force is required to maintain world order, while liberals prefer the pursuit of peace through negotiation and dialog. Conservatives are eager to preserve moral standards; liberals cherish personal autonomy.

At root, conservatives and liberals see the world so differently because they have two different conceptions of human nature. Liberals tend to believe in Rousseau's proposition that human nature is intrinsically good. Therefore they believe that people who fail or do bad things are not acting out of laziness or wickedness; rather, society put them in this unfortunate position. Since people are innately good, liberals hold, the great conflicts in the world are not the result of good versus evil; rather, they arise out of terrible misunderstandings that can be corrected through ongoing conversation and through the mediation of such groups as the United Nations. Finally, the liberal's high opinion of human nature leads to the view that if you give people autonomy they will use their freedom well.

Conservatives know better. Conservatives recognize that there are two principles in human nature—good and evil—and these are in constant conflict. Given the warped timber of humanity, conservatives seek a social structure that helps to bring out the best in human nature and suppress man's lower or base impulses. Conservatives support capitalism because it is a way of steering our natural pursuit of self-interest toward the material betterment of society at large. Conservatives insist that because there are evil régimes and destructive forces in the world that cannot be talked out of their nefarious objectives, force is an indispensable element of international relations. Finally, conservatives support autonomy when it is attached to personal responsibility—when people are held accountable for their actions—but they also believe in the indispensability of moral incubators (the family, the church, civic institutions) that are aimed at instructing people to choose virtue over vice.

I am a conservative, Chris, because I believe that conservatives have an accurate understanding of human nature and liberals do not. Since liberals have a wrong view of man, their policies are unlikely to achieve good results. Indeed, liberal programs frequently subvert liberal objectives. Richard Nixon once described the liberal Democrats as the party of "acid, amnesty, and abortion." For all its grand proclamations, today's liberalism seems to be characterized by a pathological hostility to America, to capitalism, and to traditional moral values. In short, liberalism has become the party of anti-Americanism, economic plunder, and immorality. By contrast, conservative policies are not only more likely to produce the good society, they are also the best means to achieve liberal goals such as peace, tolerance, and social justice.

2

◼ The Libertarian Temptation

Dear Chris,

I can see that you are not entirely happy with my definition of conservatism. Like a lot of young people, you have strong libertarian instincts, and you are inclined to a "leave us alone" ideology that calls for the government to stay out of your pocketbook and your private life. In policy, I generally agree. Even so, I want to point out that libertarianism is not the same thing as conservatism.

Libertarianism is a philosophy of government, but conservatism is a philosophy of life. The libertarians want to contract the domain of government to expand the domain of personal liberty. For the most part, conservatives support this. But on the question of how liberty is to be used, on the central question of what constitutes the good life, libertarianism is largely silent.

The central libertarian principle is freedom, and to defend freedom, some libertarians find themselves arguing that whatever people choose is always right. But one could arrive at this view only from the premise that human nature is so good that it is virtually flawless. In reality, human nature is flawed, and freedom is frequently used badly. Conservatives understand this. Conservatives defend freedom not because they believe in the right to do as you please, but because freedom is the precondition for virtue. It is only when people choose freely that they can choose the good. Without freedom there is no virtue: A coerced virtue is no virtue at all.

Consider an example that contrasts the conservative and libertarian views of freedom. If you said to a libertarian, "What if 300 million Americans opt to become pornographers like Larry Flynt? Would that constitute a good society?" While the conservative would emphatically answer no, the pure libertarian would have to answer yes, because these people have chosen freely. As this example illustrates, libertarianism is a philosophy of choice without political concern for what people actually choose. Thus, although many libertarians live virtuously, libertarianism as a philosophy is indifferent to virtue. In this respect it differs markedly from conservatism.

Admittedly, vast areas of programmatic agreement exist between libertarians and conservatives. Both believe that the federal government has grown prodigiously and that it needs to be severely curbed. Even on social issues, libertarians and conservatives are often on the same side, although not always for the same reasons. A few years ago, I heard a conversation between a conservative and a libertarian. The conservative said, "I am distressed by the idea of fornication in public parks." The libertarian replied, "I am distressed by the idea of public parks." And on the policy issue in question, the two found themselves in happy agreement.

Conservatives, like libertarians, resist looking to the government to redistribute income. But on some occasions, conservatives are willing to use the power of government to foster virtue. Libertarians find this appalling. "If you won't trust the government with your money," one of them said to me, "how can you trust it with your soul?" Well, nobody is putting the government in charge of morality or salvation. But government policy does influence behavior, and conservatives are not averse to using the instruments of government, such as the presidential bully pulpit or the incentive structure of the tax code, to promote decent institutions (such as intact families) and decent behavior (such as teenage sexual abstinence).

The issue that best illustrates the libertarian–conservative disagreement is the drug war. Libertarians say that the "war against drugs" has been a failure, and this seems to be true. But what if the antidrug effort could be conducted in such a way that it was a success? Libertarians would still have to oppose it because in principle they are against the idea of the government regulating drugs. Conservatives, who may agree with libertarians that our current antidrug campaign is imprudent and inefficient, would generally have no problem with a more sensible campaign that effectively reduced the use and abuse of hard drugs.

Chris, I am not asking you to relinquish your libertarian beliefs. But I think your libertarianism would be intellectually richer if it were integrated into a more comprehensive conservative philosophy that advanced a substantive vision of the good life and the good society. In other words, the best argument for freedom is not that it is an end in itself but that it is the necessary prerequisite for choosing what is right. Think about it.

3
▨ The Education of a Conservative

Dear Chris,

I am glad that you found my letters contrasting conservatism and liberalism (and distinguishing both from libertarianism) to be helpful. You pronounce yourself a "libertarian conservative," and this seems to me an excellent way to preserve your libertarian economic philosophy within a broader conservative worldview.

Let me go on to address your questions about how I became a conservative, and how I became involved with the conservative movement at Dartmouth. I arrived at Dartmouth in the fall of 1979, having come to the United States the previous year as a Rotary exchange student from Bombay, India. Dartmouth was entirely new to me. I had never visited the campus before; I am not even sure that I had heard of Dartmouth when I applied. But my host family in Arizona convinced me that it was an Ivy League institution and that I should attend. They left out the part about the snow.

I started out at Dartmouth as a pretty typical Asian American student. My plans were to major in economics and to earn an advanced degree in business, either in the United States or in London. I enjoyed writing, however, and signed up to write for the campus newspaper, the *Dartmouth*. I learned the basics of journalism and wrote several news stories during my freshman year. Toward the end of the year, a major schism occurred at "The D." The editor of the paper came out of the closet as a conservative. He began to write editorials supporting the candidacy of Ronald Reagan for president; the other editors, scandalized by this offense, began the process of getting him fired. They succeeded, and the brash young editor, Gregory Fossedal, resolved to start an alternative weekly newspaper. He called it the *Dartmouth Review*, and modeled it after William F. Buckley's *National Review*.

I was not a conservative. I had never heard of *National Review*. In fact, I didn't see myself as political. In retrospect, I realize that by the end of my freshman year my views were mostly liberal. If you had said "capitalism," I would have said "greed." If you had said "Reagan," I would have said "washed-up former actor." If you had said "El Salvador," I would have said, "another Vietnam." If you had said "morality," I would have said, "can't legislate it." These were not reasoned convictions. Rather, I was carried by the tide. A liberal current flows on most college campuses, and the more prestigious the campus, the stronger the current. If you do not recognize this, you will surely be swept along. The only way to avoid this is to actively resist the waves.

Although I had acquiesced in the prevailing liberal *weltanshauung*, I was by no means a radical. Indeed, during my freshman year I was offended by much of the radicalism on campus, but I had no coherent way to think about it or to express my dissatisfaction. For instance, during our convocation ceremony, a very dignified affair, the college chaplain said to our freshman class, "I want each of you to look to the student on your right, and the student on the left. One of the three of you will have a homosexual experience to climax before you graduate." Personally, I found this a bit shocking. Indeed, I looked to my left and right, and I resolved to avoid those two guys for the rest of my days at Dartmouth.

I was also troubled by the radicalism of the feminist professors on campus. These women made statements to the effect that all males were potential rapists. One professor said she could barely walk around the Dartmouth campus because the tall tower of Baker Library upset her so deeply. To her, the tall buildings at Dartmouth were "phallic symbols." I swear, this woman's definition of a phallic symbol was anything that was longer than it was wide. And because these women were famous for bringing their politics into the classroom, your grade was likely to suffer if you didn't agree with them.

Another phenomenon I found puzzling was the anti-Americanism of many foreign students. We had foreign students who were on full scholarship at one of the most beautiful campuses in the world, yet they spent their time bitterly complaining, and some even found Dartmouth responsible for their "institutional oppression." Iranian students who had been sent to America to study by the Shah had now become ardent supporters of the Ayatollah Khomeini, whose social policies they deplored but whose anti-Americanism they found delightful and exhilarating. At the time I did not know what to make of these things.

I joined the *Dartmouth Review* for two reasons: one esthetic, the other intellectual. The first was that I found a style and a joie de vivre that I had not previously associated with conservatism. The best example of this was the paper's mentor, Jeffrey Hart, a professor of English at Dartmouth and a senior editor of *National Review*. Hart was exactly the opposite of the conservative stereotype. He wore a long raccoon coat around campus, and he smoked long pipes with curvaceous stems. He sometimes wore buttons that said things such as "Soak the Poor." In his office he had a wooden, pincer-like device that he explained was for the purpose of "pinching women that you don't want to touch." Rumor had it that he went to faculty meetings with his wooden-hand contraption. When a dean or professor went on and on, Hart would churn the rotary device and the fingers on the wooden hand would drum impatiently in a clacking motion, as if to say, "Get on with it."

Even more outrageous than Hart's attire and equipment was his mind. He was a walking producer of aphorisms. "When I heard about the French Revolution," Hart once said, "my reaction was that I was against it." During a trip to Washington, D.C., a group of us saw an antiracism demonstration. One fiery-eyed black man wearing a Malcolm X shirt approached Hart. "Hey man," he said. "Can I have two dollars for breakfast?" Hart replied, "Shame on you. You should be using the money to fight racism."

Hart's writing was striking for its lyricism and candor. His most controversial column about Dartmouth was called "The Ugly Protesters." He wrote it during the time of the protests against white rule in South Africa, when the campus green was regularly occupied by a horde of angry young men and women shouting, "End apartheid," "Avenge the death of Steven Biko," "No more Sharpeville massacres," and "Divestment now." Hart wrote that he was puzzled by the intensity of the protesters. What possible interest could they have in events so remote from their everyday lives? Observing the protesters, Hart noted that their unifying characteristic was their state of dishevelment. Not to mince words, they were, as a group, rather ugly. Exploring the connection between their demeanor and their political activism, Hart arrived at the following conclusion: They were protesting their own ugliness! Hart's column caused a sensation on campus. Walking to class the next day, I saw a remarkable sight on the Dartmouth green.

In an attempt to disprove Hart's characterization, the protesters had shown up in suits and long dresses. But they had made a strategic blunder because their suits were so ill-fitting that they looked even more ridiculous. Watching the scene from his office in Sanborn Hall, Hart blew billows of smoke from his pipe and chuckled with obscene pleasure.

In part because of his political incorrectness, Hart was one of the few people I have met whose jokes made people laugh out loud. His sense of humor can be illustrated by a contest that *National Review* privately held among its editors following the publication of a controversial Bill Buckley column on the issue of AIDS. People were debating whether AIDS victims should be quarantined as syphilis victims had been in the past. Buckley said no: The solution was to have a small tattoo on their rear ends to warn potential partners. Buckley's suggestion caused a bit of a public stir, but the folks at *National Review* were animated by a different question: What should the tattoo say? A contest was held, and when the entries were reviewed, the winner by unanimous consent was Hart. He suggested the lines emblazoned on the gates to Dante's *Inferno:* "Abandon all hope, ye who enter here."

I remember some of those early dinners at the Hart farmhouse. We drank South American wine and listened to recordings of Ernest Hemingway and F. Scott Fitzgerald, and of Robert Frost reading his poems, and Nixon speeches, and comedian Rich Little doing his

Nixon imitation, and George C. Scott delivering the opening speech in *Patton*, and some of Winston Churchill's orations, and the music from the BBC version of Evelyn Waugh's *Brideshead Revisited*. There was an ethos here, and a sensibility, and it conveyed to me something about conservatism that I had never suspected. Here was a conservatism that was alive; that was engaged with art, music, and literature; that was at the same time ironic, lighthearted, and fun.

The second reason I joined the *Dartmouth Review* was that I was greatly impressed by the seriousness of the conservative students. They were passionate about ideas, and they argued vigorously about what it meant to be a conservative, and what it meant to be an American, and who was a liberally educated person, and who should belong to a liberal arts community, and whether journalism could be objective, and whether reason could refute revelation, and whether corporations should give money to charity, and why Joseph Stalin was a worse man than Adolf Hitler, and why socialism was not merely inefficient but also immoral. Once, in the middle of a serious argument, I proposed a break for dinner and was greeted with the response, "We haven't resolved the morality of U.S. foreign policy and you want to EAT?"

I realized that these students, who were not much older than I was, had answers before I had figured out what the questions were. Their conversations, peppered with references to classical and modern sources, revealed how much I could learn from them, and how much I had to learn on my own. Thus I began to read voraciously, not just my classroom stuff but also Edmund Burke, David Hume, Adam Smith, F. Scott Fitzgerald, Evelyn Waugh, Friedrich Hayek, and Aleksandr Solzhenitsyn. Gradually, I found myself developing a grounded point of view. For the first time, disparate facts began to fit together, to make sense. Conservatism provided me with a framework, durable and yet flexible, for understanding the world. And having understood the world, at the tender age of twenty, I was ready to change it.

4
Pig Wrestling at Dartmouth

Dear Chris,

While I was at the *Dartmouth Review*, we used to tell the deans that taking on our campus paper was like wrestling with a pig. Not only did it get everyone dirty, but the pig liked it!

You have pressed me for further details about my Dartmouth escapades, and I am happy to oblige. As I recount some of the sophomoric things we did, I ask you to keep in mind that during this time we were sophomores! Having turned forty a year ago, I now have a somewhat different perspective than I had when I was twenty. Thus in bringing back those happy and adventurous times, it seems worthwhile to ask what we accomplished. What did we gain and what did we lose, and was it worth it?

The first thing I should note is that we were an outrageous bunch. I didn't start out this way; in fact, for the first year I was considered a moderating influence on the *Dartmouth Review*. The reason I became radicalized is that I saw how harshly the conservative newspaper was treated by professors and by the administration. No sooner had the first issue appeared on campus than the administration threatened to sue the *Dartmouth Review* for using the name "Dartmouth." The college maintained that it owned full and exclusive copyright to the name. Never mind that Dartmouth is a town in England. In fact, some two dozen establishments in Hanover—from Dartmouth Bookstore to Dartmouth Cleaners to Dartmouth Printing—all used the name. These were commercial operations unaffiliated with the college. By contrast, we were a group of Dartmouth students publishing a weekly about Dartmouth College and distributing it to the Dartmouth community. Clearly the motive of the lawsuit was ideological.

The administration did not stop with legal threats. Early in the paper's history, one of the editors, Ben Hart, was distributing copies to the Blunt Alumni Center, when a college official named Sam Smith went berserk, attacked Ben, and bit him! It happened this way: Smith grabbed Ben from behind, Ben attempted to free himself by wrapping his arm around Smith's neck, and Smith proceeded to bite him on the chest. When Ben—who is the son of Jeffrey Hart—entered his dad's office and explained the bloody gash, his father's terse response was, "Thank God you didn't have him in a scissors hold." Smith was eventually convicted of assault and paid a small fine.

These actions, inconsequential and even amusing in themselves, nevertheless reveal the psychology of the typical liberal college administrator. These guys are harsh, even brutal, in dealing with conservative dissent; invertebrate, even encouraging, in dealing with liberal dissent—and yet they solemnly insist that they are fair and unbiased. During my freshman year, the Dartmouth administration sought to expel a reporter from the *Dartmouth Review* for "vexatious oral exchange" with a professor. Meanwhile, the left-wing radicals who took over the Dartmouth library faced no charges, and Dartmouth's president even apologized for being out of town at the time and unable to attend to their urgent demands. As this hollow man explained himself to the radicals, "My absence was not an attempt to be insensitive to your burning need."

These incidents point to the larger dilemma facing conservative students in a liberal culture. The dilemma can be stated this way. Typically, the conservative attempts to conserve, to hold on to the values of the existing society. But what if the existing society is liberal? What if the existing society is inherently hostile to conservative beliefs? It is foolish for a conservative to attempt to conserve that culture. Rather, he must seek to undermine it, to thwart it, to destroy it at the root level. This means that the conservative must stop being conservative. More precisely, he must be philosophically conservative but temperamentally radical. This is what we at the *Dartmouth Review* quickly understood.

I discovered another reason why the conservative activist on the liberal campus needs a radical approach. At Dartmouth and other liberal campuses, politics is frequently transmitted to the students not through argument but through etiquette. You see, the high school graduate who goes to an elite college such as Dartmouth wants nothing more than to learn what it means to be an educated Dartmouth man (or woman). And the professors realize this, and exploit it. Consider the freshman who goes to a faculty cocktail party and says that he is concerned about "the Communist plot in Nicaragua." What do the professors do? Do they argue with him? Do they seek to demonstrate that the Sandinistas are not Marxist? No, they raise their noses into the air and give the student a look as if to say, "Are you from Iowa?" The student is humiliated. He realizes that he has committed a social gaffe. And over time, he learns. By the time he is a senior he is winning big social accolades from his professors by going on about "the rising tide of homophobia that is engulfing our society."

At the *Dartmouth Review*, we recognized that to confront liberalism fully we could not be content with rebutting liberal arguments. We also had to subvert liberal culture, and this meant disrupting the etiquette of liberalism. In other words, we had to become social guerillas. And this we set out to do with a vengeance.

Reading over old issues of the *Review*, and sharing recollections with my former colleagues, I am sometimes amazed to realize what social and intellectual renegades we were. We were not above using *ad hominem* attacks. We described one professor as sporting "a polyester tie and a rat's-hair mustache." When he wrote to complain, noting that he never wore polyester ties and that his mustache could not reasonably be compared to rat's hair, we printed an apology. "We Goofed, see p. 6." In our apology, we said, "We regret our error. In reality Professor Spitzer has a rat's-hair tie and a polyester mustache."

Feminists and homosexuals were a regular target of *Review* satire. One of our columnists, Keeney Jones, observed a decade after Dartmouth went coed, "The question is not whether women should be educated at Dartmouth. The question is whether women should be educated at all." The *Review* also printed an alumnus's Solomonic observation that "any man who thinks a woman is his intellectual equal is probably right." And the Last Word—a series of quips and quotations on the last page of the newspaper—featured the observation: "Homosexuality is fine," said Bill, half in Ernest.

Sometimes items from the bad-taste file at *National Review* made their way into the *Dartmouth Review*. You see, the editors of *National Review* sometimes make jokes that are too inflammatory for a respectable national magazine to print. But we found them entirely appropriate for a college weekly. Thus the *Dartmouth Review*'s obituary for actress Natalie Wood ended thus, "We deplore the foul rumor. Ted Kennedy was not on Catalina Island when Natalie Wood drowned." When the new Miss America, Vanessa Williams, was forced to give up her title following news reports that she had posed nude for *Penthouse*, the *Dartmouth Review* noted, "Jesse Jackson may pull out of the presidential race this season. It has been revealed that his grandmother has been posing nude in *National Geographic*."

That some of these quips are in bad taste goes without saying. But is this scorched-earth approach effective? Let's consider a couple of examples. When Dartmouth refused to stop funding the Gay Students Association, despite numerous *Review* editorials questioning why funds should be awarded based on sexual orientation, we decided to test the consistency of the administration's policy. We founded the Dartmouth Bestiality Society. We appointed a president, a vice president, a treasurer, and a zookeeper. We wrote up an application and developed a budget. Then we went before the college committee on funding and made our case.

The administrators were appalled, of course. "There is no interest in, *ahem*, bestiality at Dartmouth," one said. To which the president of the Bestiality Society gamely replied, "That may be true, Dean Hanson, but it is because of centuries of discrimination! Those of us who are inclined toward animals have been systematically excluded and ostracized. Our organization will provide a supportive atmosphere in which people of our particular sexual orientation are treated with respect. At Dartmouth, if not in society, let us put an end to beastophobia."

No, we didn't get recognition or funding. But we did make our point, and the point was well covered in the local media. One newspaper printed a hilarious feature titled, "Students Go to the Dogs."

Another of our escapades involved the Indian symbol. Dartmouth had banned the Indian symbol as offensive to Indians. We sent out a survey to more than a hundred Indian tribes across the country and included a picture of the Indian symbol. The tribes were asked to decide whether they found the symbol offensive. When the results came back, we found that most tribes *loved* the symbol. The vast majority wanted Dartmouth to retain it, and some tribes had even voted on the issue. When we published the results of our poll, a long silence ensued in Hanover. The administration had grown so used to trotting out the head of the Native American Studies department that it trusted his views could be taken as representative of the Indian population. But we had demonstrated pretty conclusively that it was not so. When *Fortune* magazine published an article on our exposé, we were emboldened to try other stunts. One of them was to pay a local company to fly a plane over the playing fields during Dartmouth's football games. The plane dragged a huge banner that said GO DARTMOUTH INDIANS. The students cheered, and the administration was furious; but there was little the deans could do.

Our greatest success was undoubtedly the Cole incident. Professor William Cole was a black music professor who seemed to have been hired to fulfill affirmative action requirements. He was given tenure despite his virtually nonexistent publication record. His specialty was racial and political diatribes laced with obscenities, which he delivered in class in a kind of street dialect. In short, Professor Cole was a God-given opportunity for the *Dartmouth Review*.

We sent a reporter to Cole's class during the first two weeks of the semester, when students are allowed to audit courses and no attendance is taken. Our reporter taped Cole's diatribes, which appeared in the paper under the title, "Bill Cole's Song-and-Dance Routine." Cole described white students as "honkies," women as "pussies," and he praised a man who had tried to blow up the Washington Monument as an enlightened opponent of a racist society. These statements were direct quotations, and they were on tape. The article produced a sensation on campus.

The Dartmouth faculty rushed to Cole's defense. They passed a resolution denouncing the *Dartmouth Review*, the first of many, I might add. In the resolution, the faculty pointed out that they had full academic freedom to teach as they wished, and they accused us of trampling on that freedom. The officers of the *Dartmouth Review* responded by passing a resolution denouncing the Dartmouth faculty. We noted in our resolution that while they had the academic freedom to teach, we had the First Amendment right to criticize their teaching.

Incensed by our article, Cole sued the *Dartmouth Review*. He claimed that his reputation had been trashed, which of course it had. He wanted several million dollars.

The only problem with Cole's suit was that truth is an incontrovertible defense against libel. Cole never alleged that our article was inaccurate, only that it had shown him to be a fool. Our position was that he was, in fact, a fool. And the court apparently agreed, because it dismissed his lawsuit. Cole then turned to the Dartmouth administration for help. But what could they do? Disgusted, Cole resigned his tenured position at the college. The last I heard, he had opened a drum store somewhere in Vermont.

The Cole story, however, was not quite at an end. Cole's wife, Sarah Sully, who is white, was a tenured professor of French at Dartmouth. She assigned her class a paper in which students were asked to give their assessment of the *Dartmouth Review*. Because most of the students knew that Sully was married to Cole, they submitted papers very critical of the conservative newspaper. But one student who didn't know who Sarah Sully was, wrote in French that he enjoyed reading the *Dartmouth Review* and often agreed with it. When this student got his paper back, his grade was a C. He showed it to a few friends, and they suggested he go to the head of the department. The head of the department, a fair man, convened a committee of three professors, who gave the paper a B. Sarah Sully was then ordered to change the student's grade. She refused, and resigned her tenured position at the college.

As a consequence of such escapades, the *Dartmouth Review* became nationally famous. Of course, we were regularly denounced by the *New York Times* and other publications. But our editors did appear in *Newsweek* and on ABC's *Nightline*. Our exploits were praised by conservative magazines and by the editorial page of the *Wall Street Journal*. Many Dartmouth alumni found out about the administration's misdoings through these national channels, and Dartmouth's president was the chagrined recipient of numerous phone calls that began, "What the hell is going on up there?" Eventually, the *Dartmouth Review*'s influence spread to other campuses: Inspired by our example, conservative students at some fifty other colleges started alternative newspapers, many of which are still around. The spark we kindled has become an enduring flame.

Now that I can look back at the *Dartmouth Review* with some perspective, I see that it accomplished four major objectives. First, it trained a whole group of young conservatives in journalism and activism. Some of these have gone on to distinguished careers in politics. One of our editors, Peter Robinson, wrote Ronald Reagan's Berlin Wall speech, "Mr. Gorbachev, tear down this wall." Another, Laura Ingraham, is a regular pundit on radio and television. Ben Hart published a successful book about his Dartmouth exploits and now runs a large direct-mail company that raises funds for political candidates. Greg Fossedal wrote editorials for the *Wall Street Journal* before joining a money market research firm and settling down to father six kids. Keeney Jones wrote speeches for Bill Bennett and is now a Catholic priest.

None of these people would have taken these pathways if they had not worked for the *Dartmouth Review*.

Second, the *Review* was, and remains, a valuable check on the excesses of the Dartmouth faculty and administration. Over the years, the newspaper's exposés have forced the administration to abandon many a cherished liberal program. Who knows what other outrages the administration might have perpetrated had the *Review* not been around? As Professor Hart has said, thanks to the *Review*, "Dartmouth is no longer a place where the liberal sheep can graze unmolested."

Third, the newspaper generated lively discussion at Dartmouth about a whole slate of issues that would not otherwise have been talked about. Even the paper's critics admitted this. As the *New Republic* editorialized, "The *Dartmouth Review* has succeeded where countless tenured professors have failed" in fostering ongoing debates on campus about free speech, affirmative action, the liberal arts, and politics.

Finally, the *Review* moved the political center at Dartmouth decisively to the right. When I return to Dartmouth now and ask a typical student, "What are your politics?" the reply is, "Well, I'm a moderate conservative. I voted for Bush, but I am not as right-wing as those guys on the *Dartmouth Review*." What this student does not recognize is that it is the influence of the *Dartmouth Review* over the years that has enabled him to say that. Moderate conservatism was totally outside the pale when the newspaper was founded. But by staking out a kind of far-right position, the *Review* has legitimized a wide range of positions in the middle.

I learned a lot at Dartmouth, and I consider my tenure at the *Dartmouth Review* to be central to my learning experience. In fact, the last time I got a call from my class agent reminding me of how much my Dartmouth education had benefited my career and asking me to contribute to my alma mater, I told him, "Mike, I already have. I sent a check last week to the *Dartmouth Review*."

5
▓ Fighting Political Correctness

Dear Chris,

In your reaction to my Dartmouth stories, I detect a hint of envy. You complain that the conservatives on your campus are a sorry bunch: Many don't want to be publicly identified as conservative, some are too busy with academic work, others shy away from controversy. We had these same problems, but we overcame them by developing a guerilla strategy that was as effective as it was fun. Do the same, Chris, and you, too, will have people tracking you down to find out how they can get involved.

Where to start? I don't know. Conduct a survey to find out how many professors in the religion department believe in God. Distribute a pamphlet titled "Feminist Thought" that is made up of blank pages. Establish a So ciety for Creative Homophobia. Prepare a freshmen course guide that lists your college's best, and worst, professors. Publish Maya Angelou's poems alongside a bunch of meaningless doggerel and see whether anyone can tell the difference. Put a picture of death-row inmate Mumia Abu-Jamal on your Web site and instruct people who think he deserves capital punishment to click a button and execute him online. Whew, I better stop with these suggestions before I get too carried away.

In a more serious tone, let me address your question about how the current situation on campus differs from what I experienced as an undergraduate. "Is political correctness alive and well?" you ask. "And if so, have your efforts to fight this monster been in vain? How do we fight it more effectively?"

The first assault against political correctness came in the early 1990s. My book *Illiberal Education* was, as you note, the first book-length expose. Actually, I began that study quite by chance. I had just finished two years with the Reagan administration and had come to the American Enterprise Institute as a young scholar. Soon after I arrived, in January 1989, I had lunch with Morton Kondracke, a Dartmouth alumnus. I was telling Kondracke about some of the outrages being perpetrated at Dartmouth, but he was skeptical. "It's hard to believe that this stuff is really going on," he said.

"I know," I told him. "We're having a hard time convincing some of our alumni supporters. They refuse to believe that the left is that crazy."

"Are these things unique to Dartmouth," Kondracke asked, "or are they typical of what is happening at campuses across the country?"

I confessed that I did not know.

"Well, *there's* your book idea," Kondracke said. "Go and find out."

I did, and the result was *Illiberal Education*. My research for that book was helped immeasurably by two things: I was young and could masquerade as a student; and I was a "person of color" and could masquerade as a radical. No sooner did I walk into radical meetings at campuses such as Berkeley and Harvard than the minority activists drew me into their confidence. Their attitude was, "Welcome, brother. Let us show you the blueprints of our revolution."

Illiberal Education was published in 1991. The argument of the book, perfectly captured by the title, was that universities profess to be "liberal" while acting in grossly "illiberal" ways. Actually, I hesitated until the last minute about the title. The book had already gone through several titles. When I began the project, Professor Hart jokingly suggested that I call it *Bend Over, America*. And so this became the working title for the duration of my research.

Although I am often credited with inventing the term *political correctness*, I did nothing more than to help publicize it. It is an old Marxist term, once used between Stalinists and Trotskyites to determine who was "politically correct" from the Marxist point of view. The term had been revived during the 1980s to describe policies and attitudes that were congruent with liberal orthodoxy. When I first heard it, I thought the campus activists who bandied the phrase around were being ironic. But when I saw that these ideologues were deadly serious, I realized that a new form of repression was being advocated in the name of liberation.

Illiberal Education employed a strategy that had been used to great effect by the *Dartmouth Review:* that of embarrassing people by quoting them. Ridicule is a powerful political weapon, and it is all the more deadly if it can be deployed by using the target's own words. The effectiveness of that book was largely a result of its irrefutable documented incidents and tabulated quotations. So no matter how much the leftists and the multiculturalists claimed that I had wrongly described the situation on campus, they could not deny that the things described in my book took place. This, by itself, was crushing. Thus the countless "refutations" of *Illiberal Education* bounced off me lightly. When the *Village Voice* put me on its cover along with the title WANTED: FOR INTELLECTUAL FRAUD, I was greatly flattered and, to this day, I have that cover on the wall in my office.

The conservative critique of political correctness, which I articulated along with Bill Bennett, Lynne Cheney, Roger Kimball, and others, had the beneficial effect of splitting the classical or old-line liberals from the left. The difference between the two groups may be illustrated by their attitudes toward free speech. Classical liberals believe in free speech because they are confident that, in a clash between truth and error, truth will prevail. The left does not believe in free speech. Of course, the leftists are happy to invoke the principle of free speech when one of their own guys is being threatened. Once they are in power, however, leftists are perfectly comfortable with suppressing the views of those they abhor. The leftist principle was stated by Herbert Marcuse in the 1960s: No free speech for fascists!

In the name of this doctrine, the left had for years been shouting down its opponents. During the 1980s, left-wing activists prevented national security adviser Jeane Kirkpatrick, Nicaraguan contra leader Adolfo Calero, and several others from speaking on campus. Many colleges even had "speech codes"; these had the effect of outlawing candid debate on sensitive topics such as affirmative action. One such code even outlawed "inappropriately directed laughter." These codes were necessary, the champions of political correctness argued, to protect the self-image of minority students. Ironically, censorship was being practiced in the name of "diversity."

As a result of the conservative expose of political correctness, many old-line liberals began to criticize speech codes, and soon the courts began to intervene and strike those codes down as inconsistent with the First Amendment. Now, as far as I am aware, no college actually enforces its speech code, although several still have one on the books. This is one area in which the critique of political correctness has been successful. I don't just mean that the official codes have been suspended; I also mean that the parameters of acceptable debate have been greatly widened. Topics that could scarcely have been brought up a decade ago can now be addressed, and I address them all the time during my frequent lectures on campus.

Another great success of the P.C. critique is that it has helped mitigate the national influence of university ideologues such as Noam Chomsky, Andrew Ross, Eve Sedgwick, and Molefi Asante. Many of these radicals were the "public intellectual" darlings of the late eighties and early nineties. They were regularly featured on television, their articles routinely appearing in the *New York Review of Books* and the *New Yorker.* Their views were considered significant in shaping enlightened public opinion. But the conservative exposé of the narrowness and intolerance of these ideologues subjected many of them to intense national ridicule, and it has largely cut them off from having a broad cultural influence. Every now and then, one of the radicals surfaces to make some outlandish claim, is greeted either by indifference or by ridicule, and promptly ducks out of public sight.

On campus, the influence of the radicals remains strong. Despite the demise of the speech codes, multiculturalism and political correctness are still powerful forces to contend with. When I was a freshman at Dartmouth, there were two types of professors. The first group was made up of old-line liberals; they usually wore jackets and ties and spoke in an elegant, formal tone. Then there were the radicals whose politics were shaped in the 1960s. These professors wore informal clothing, wanted to be addressed by their first names, and used such words as "shit" in class. The radicals had their ideological agenda; but at least they were balanced by the old-line liberals, who believed in such things as high academic standards, teaching the classics, and maintaining the basic canons of civility.

Now, however, the old-line liberals are gone and, on many campuses across the country, the generation of the 1960s is fully in charge. Today's deans and professors come overwhelmingly from this group. While a few have abandoned their old commitments, in general the intellectuals of this generation continue to espouse a worldview that took shape during their formative years. It is not hard to discover that ethos by reading what these fellows wrote in the 1960s and 1970s. Many of them predicted that capitalism would disintegrate, that its inner contradictions would be exposed. These savants expected guerilla revolutions of a Marxist stripe to break out all over the world. The future, they were convinced, lay in models adopted in Stalin's Russia, or Mao's China, or Castro's Cuba, or Ortega's Nicaragua.

Well, history has proved unkind to such prophecies. And now many from this sixties-generation are distressed to see that the world has moved dramatically in a conservative direction. Even worse, the professors know that they are in no position to reverse these trends. They can't put the Berlin Wall back up. They can't restore the Sandinistas to power in Nicaragua. They have no hope of stopping the powerful current of economic globalization. "But hey," the professor at Oberlin College consoles himself, "at least here I can take over the English department." So what we are seeing is a desperate effort on the part of the radicals to control their own environment, to dominate their fetid little ponds, to impose their political values on a new generation of students.

What can be done about this? Well, probably the best hope lies in the actuarial tables. The radicals now have tenure, and in one sense we simply have to wait until they die off. In the meantime, however, there are many ways to fight this entrenched group.

The best way to defeat political correctness is to expose its lies. Basically, P.C. is about pretending, about publicly insisting that something is true when we know privately that it isn't, about shutting down people who won't conform to the prevailing orthodoxy. Thus the three canonical principles of political correctness are to deny the relevant differences between racial groups, between men and women, and between heterosexuals and homosexuals. The observation that young black males have a higher violent crime rate than young white males is dismissed as a "stereotype," even though a mountain of empirical data supports it. The military is relentlessly pressured by feminist groups to pretend that women are just as strong physically as men. Homosexual activists assure us, with straight faces, that "AIDS is an equal opportunity killer." And so on, fiction upon fiction, the entire edifice relying for its stability on people's fear that if they speak the truth they will first be accused of racism and then hounded and penalized. One has to be brave to defy these taboos and threats, and that is why one of the most important qualities needed among campus conservatives is courage.

Affirmative action has become a clinical sample of political correctness because many of its advocates now recognize that the only way to defend it is to lie about it. A few years ago, a law student who worked in the Georgetown University admissions department wrote an article for the campus newspaper revealing large differences in the grades and standardized test scores of blacks and whites admitted to Georgetown Law School. African American students with lower scores were routinely admitted, and white students with better scores were routinely turned away. Confronted with the data, the dean of the law school, Judith Areen, denied that merit principles were being compromised. "We don't just measure a student's ability with grades and test scores," she indignantly asserted. "We also use other factors."

But in a speech at Georgetown Law School, I challenged her to provide me with a list of those "other factors." Presumably those factors referred to extracurricular talents. I was eager to have her specify those extracurricular talents, because, whatever they were, clearly no white students possessed them; whites were never admitted to the law school with the same low scores that proved adequate for black students. Needless to say, the dean did not respond to my challenge. But her silence did not go unnoticed by the students.

While there are some risks for students in fighting political correctness, these risks are, in my view, well worth taking. After all, there are few ways in which a student can make a greater contribution to strengthening the prospects for free inquiry and open debate on campus. A defeat for political correctness is, quite simply, a victory for truth and freedom of mind.

6
Authentic vs. Bogus Multiculturalism

Dear Chris,

I remember, during my first year at Dartmouth, going to meetings sponsored by the International Students Association. I enjoyed these meetings because they presented a fine opportunity to eat good ethnic food. It was in these venues that I first encountered that most intriguing creature, the multiculturalist. The multiculturalist that I remember most vividly was a white guy who wore a pony-tail and a Nehru jacket. He was visibly excited to meet a fellow from India.

"So you're from India," he said. "What a great country."

"Have you ever been there?" I asked.

"No," he confessed. "But I've always wanted to go."

"Why?" I asked, genuinely curious.

"I don't know," he said. "It's just—so liberating!"

Because I had a happy childhood in India, I have many nice things to say about my native country, but if I had to choose one word to describe life there, I probably wouldn't choose "liberating." I decided to prod my enthusiastic acquaintance a little.

"What is it that you find so liberating about India?" I asked. "Could it be the caste system? Dowry? Arranged marriage?"

My purpose was to challenge him, to generate a discussion. But at this point he lost interest. My question ran into a wall of indifference.

"Got to get another drink," he said, racing toward the bar.

I tried the same experiment several times, always with a similar result. And as I reflected on the matter, a thought occurred to me. Maybe these students weren't really so interested in India after all. Maybe they were projecting their domestic discontents with their parents, their preachers, or their country onto the faraway land of India. Maybe they imagined India to be something that she was not: a land of social liberation, where conventional restraints were completely lifted. While I sympathized to some degree with these aspirations, I also resented this exploitation of India for political ends. "You are entitled to your illusions," I wanted to tell the pony-tailed guy, "but India simply is not like that."

I mention this anecdote because it was an early indication of a phenomenon I was to investigate later, the phenomenon of bogus multiculturalism.

The multicultural challenge is one that conservatives must meet because it is central to what a university is all about. Multiculturalism is a movement to transform the curriculum and change the way things are taught in our schools and universities. Some people think that its triumph is inevitable. Thus sociologist Nathan Glazer a few years ago wrote a book called *We Are All Multiculturalists Now*. Glazer is not entirely enthusiastic about multiculturalism. He is convinced, however, that because America has become so racially diverse, multiculturalism is unavoidable. Glazer's mistake is to confuse the *fact* of the multiracial society with the *ideology* of multiculturalism. The two are quite distinct, and the latter is not necessarily the best way to respond to the former.

To understand the multicultural debate, it may be helpful to begin with Allan Bloom's *The Closing of the American Mind*. Bloom argued that American students are shockingly ignorant of the basic ingredients of their own Western civilization. Even graduates of the best colleges and universities have a very poor comprehension of the thinkers and ideas that have shaped their culture. Thus Ivy League graduates know that Homer wrote the *Odyssey*, and that Aquinas lived during the Middle Ages, and that Max Weber's name is pronounced with a "V." But most of them aren't sure whether the Renaissance came before the Reformation; they couldn't tell you what was going on in Britain during the French Revolution; and they look bewildered if you ask them why the American founders considered representative democracy an improvement over the kind of direct democracy that the Athenians had. Bloom concluded that even "educated" Americans were not really educated at all.

Bloom's ideas came under fierce assault, and leading the charge were proponents of multiculturalism. Multiculturalism is, as the name suggests, a doctrine of culture. Advocates of multiculturalism, such as literary critic Cornel West and historian Ronald Takaki, say that for too long the curriculum in our schools and colleges has focused exclusively on Western culture. In short, it is "Eurocentric." The problem, multiculturalists say, is not that students are insufficiently exposed to the Western perspective; it is that the Western perspective is all they are exposed to. What is needed, multiculturalists insist, is an expansion of perspectives to include minority and non-Western cultures. This is especially vital, in their view, because we are living in an interconnected global culture and there are increasing numbers of black, Hispanic, and Asian faces in the classroom. Multiculturalism presents itself as an attempt to give all students a more complete and balanced education.

Stated this way, multiculturalism seems unobjectionable and uncontroversial. It is controversial because there is a powerful political thrust behind the way multiculturalism works in practice. To discover this ideological thrust, we must look at multicultural programs as they are actually taught. Several years ago, I did my first study of a multicultural curriculum at Stanford University. I pored over the reading list, looking for the great works of non-Western culture: the *Quran*, the *Ramayana*, the *Analects* of Confucius, the *Tale of Genji*, the *Gitanjali*, and so on. But they were nowhere to be found. As I sat in on classes, I found myself presented with a picture of non-Western cultures that was unrecognizable to me as a person who had grown up in one of those cultures. Our typical reading consisted of works such as *I, Rigoberta Menchu*, the autobiography of a young Marxist feminist activist from Guatemala.

Now I don't mean to understate the importance of Guatemalan Marxist feminism as a global theme. But were students encountering the best literary output of Latin American culture? Did *I, Rigoberta Menchu* even represent the culture of Guatemala? The answer to these questions was no and no. So why were Stanford students being exposed to this stuff?

It is impossible to understand multiculturalism in America without realizing that it arises from the powerful conviction that bigotry and oppression define Western civilization in general and America in particular. The targets of this maltreatment are, of course, minorities, women, and homosexuals. And so the multiculturalists look abroad, hoping to find in other countries a better alternative to the bigoted and discriminatory ways of the West.

And what do they find? If they look honestly, they soon discover that other cultures are even more bigoted than those of the West. Ethnocentrism and discrimination are universal; it is the doctrine of equality of rights under the law that is uniquely Western. Women are treated quite badly in most non-Western cultures: Think of such customs as the veil, female foot-binding, clitoral mutilation, the tossing of females onto the pyres of their dead husbands. When I was a boy, I heard the saying, "I asked the Burmese why, after centuries of following their men, the women now walk in front. He explained that there were many unexploded land mines since the war." This is intended half-jokingly, but only half-jokingly. It conveys an attitude toward women that is fairly widespread in Asia, Africa, and South America. As for homosexuality, it is variously classified as an illness or a crime in most non-Western cultures. The Chinese, for example, have a longstanding policy of administering shock treatment to homosexuals, a practice that one government official credits with a "high cure rate."

Of course, non-Western cultures have produced many classics and great books, and these are eminently worthy of study. But not surprisingly, those classics frequently convey the same unenlightened views of minorities and women that the multiculturalists deplore in the West. The *Quran*, for instance, is the central spiritual document of one of the world's great religions, but one cannot read it without finding there a clear doctrine of male superiority. The *Tale of Genji*, the Japanese classic of the eleventh century, is a story of hierarchy, of ritual, of life at the court: It is far removed from the Western ideal of egalitarianism. The Indian classics—the *Vedas*, the *Bhagavad Gita,* and so on, are celebrations of transcendental virtues: They are a rejection of materialism, of atheism, perhaps even of the separation of church and state.

What I am saying is that non-Western cultures, and the classics that they have produced, are for the most part politically incorrect.

This poses a grave problem for American multiculturalists. One option for them is to confront non-Western cultures and to denounce them as being even more backward and retrograde than the West. But this option is politically unacceptable because non-Western cultures are viewed as historically abused and victimized. In the eyes of the multiculturalists, they deserve not criticism but affirmation. And so the multiculturalists prefer the second option: Ignore the representative traditions of non-Western cultures, pass over their great works, and focus instead on marginal and isolated works that are carefully selected to cater to Western leftist prejudices about the non-Western world.

There is a revealing section of *I, Rigoberta Menchu* in which young Rigoberta proclaims herself a *quadruple* victim of oppression. She is a person of color, and she is oppressed by racism. She is a woman, and she is oppressed by sexism. She is a Latin American, and she is oppressed by the North Americans. And finally, she is of Indian extraction, and she is oppressed by people of Spanish descent within Latin America. Here, then, is the secret of Rigoberta's curricular appeal. She is not representative of the culture or the great works of Latin America, but she *is* representative of the politics of Stanford professors. Rigoberta is, for them, a kind of model to hold up to students, especially female and minority students; like her, they, too, can think of themselves as oppressed.

This is what I call bogus multiculturalism. It is bogus because it views non-Western cultures through the ideological lens of Western leftist politics. Non-Western cultures are routinely mutilated and distorted to serve Western ideological ends. No serious understanding between cultures is possible with multiculturalism of this sort.

The alternative, in my view, is not to go back to the traditional curriculum focused on the Western classics. Rather, it is to develop an authentic multiculturalism that teaches the greatest works of Western and non-Western cultures. Matthew Arnold penned a resonant phrase: "The best that has been thought and said." That sums up the essence of a sound liberal arts curriculum. Probably Arnold had in mind the best of Western thought and culture. There is no reason in principle, however, that Arnold's criterion cannot be applied to non-Western cultures as well.

Personally, I would like to see liberal arts colleges devote the better part of the freshman year to grounding students in the classics of Western and non-Western civilization. Yes, I am talking about requirements. To heck with electives: Seventeen-year-olds don't know enough to figure out what they need to learn. Once students have been thoroughly grounded in the classics, they have three more years to choose their majors and experiment with courses in Bob Dylan and Maya Angelou. My hope, of course, is that after a year of Socrates and Confucius and Tolstoy and Tagore most students will have lost interest in Bob Dylan and Maya Angelou.

7

What's So Great
About Great Books

Dear Chris,

I see that I have gotten ahead of myself. You are a pre-med student, and you profess to be confused by all this liberal arts talk. I take it that you understand the importance of politics—it provides the necessary infrastructure for us to live peaceful, prosperous, and good lives. But you are puzzled by my emphasis on the importance of books, especially books written a long time ago. I even detect a hint of sympathy for the liberal view that Sophocles, John Milton, and William Shakespeare are just a bunch of "dead white men." Why should we read them instead of others? What do they have to say to us today? Your letter is full of questions, and they are good ones, so let me try to take them one by one. I have taken the liberty of reformulating them slightly so that they correspond to the questions that multiculturalists frequently ask.

"What, really, is a classic and why should we read so-called classics?" Samuel Johnson provides the answer in his *Preface to Shakespeare*. A classic, he writes, is a work that has survived the provinciality of its own moment in space and in time. If Shakespeare, who wrote in Elizabethan times, continues to appeal to Victorian and modern readers, and to readers outside England, it must be because he addresses universal themes, and in an appealing and enduring way. The literary critic Northrop Frye put it a little differently: A classic is simply "a work that refuses to go away."

"Even so, why is it important for students to know about a bunch of great books?" It is less important for students to learn *about* the great books than it is for them to learn *from* the great books. The great books are about fundamental human questions; indeed, they are a kind of extended argument about these questions. The philosopher Leo Strauss writes, "Liberal education consists in listening to the conversation among the greatest minds. But here we are confronted with the overwhelming difficulty that this conversation does not take place without our help—that in fact we must bring about that conversation. The greatest minds utter monologs . . . and they contradict one another regarding the most important matters. . . . We must transform their monologs into dialogs."

As Strauss suggests, this is not an easy process, but it is one that can be learned through effort, and the effort is worth it because the result is wonderfully illuminating.

Once again, the goal is not to give students a cocktail-party familiarity with a canon of great works. Indeed, Allan Bloom says it is better that students should be deeply excited, even have their lives changed, by *one* book. So if you want to embark on this journey, Chris, begin by choosing a writer who really speaks to you, such as Plato or Rousseau. That will get you started on what, I assure you, will be the most exhilarating and long-lasting adventure of your life.

"What is the point of having a static curriculum? Shouldn't the curriculum change?" Yes, and the curriculum has always changed. When *Moby Dick* was first published, the book was a failure. One reviewer complained that it was a rather lengthy account of whaling practices in Boston. *Silas Marner* was once assigned in most great book courses in America. But in time, *Moby Dick*'s literary stock went up and *Silas Marner*'s went down. Today, *Silas Marner* is considered a derivative work, but *Moby Dick* is regarded as a great book. So curricula do change. But the basis for changing them has always been judgments of merit. What is new is that multiculturalists are seeking changes in the curriculum not based on merit but based on representation. They don't argue that Rigoberta Menchu is better than Dante; their argument relies primarily on the fact that Dante was a white male and Rigoberta is a Guatemalan female. This is no basis for choosing great works or for giving students a good education.

"Shouldn't people know something about other cultures?" Yes, but it is even more important that they understand the foundations of their own culture, especially when their own culture is shaping the modern world. If you met an educated fellow from China who had never heard of Confucius but was an expert on Mark Twain, this would be odd. People are expected to have a basic comprehension of their own culture. Similarly, American students should be reasonably well versed in the *Federalist Papers*, they should know the arguments that led to the Civil War, they should be familiar with the New Deal and the Great Society, they should be acquainted with Ralph Waldo Emerson, Walt Whitman, and F. Scott Fitzgerald. Otherwise they will remain aliens in their own civilization.

"But what does Western culture have to say to blacks and other minorities?" Western culture is the only culture to take diversity seriously. Only in the West has there been a serious questioning of ethnocentrism, of the notion that "my way is the best way." The Greeks were ethnocentric, in a fashion, but their greatest thinkers realized that truth is the property of no culture. The Greeks were interested in diversity not for its own sake, and certainly not to affirm the self-esteem of anyone. The Greeks didn't have, for example, Persian History Month. But the Greeks studied other cultures because they wanted to discover what is universally true about human nature. The Greeks recognized that human nature comes draped in the garb of culture and convention. Only by carefully and critically examining other cultures in relation to their own could the Greeks hope to discover what peoples had in common, and how they differed. The Greeks investigated the evident diversity of cultures to uncover the hidden truths about human nature.

"Give me an example of a Western classic that has something to say to a black man." I can think of several, but let me give the example of Shakespeare's *Othello*. Allan Bloom wrote a wonderful essay on this play for a book he co-authored with Harry Jaffa, *Shakespeare's Politics*. In Bloom's reading, which I am following here, *Othello* is a play about a dark-skinned man, a Moor, who is trying to become a full citizen of Venice. The problem is that Venice is a relatively closed society, an ethnocentric society, and it does not easily grant membership and recognition to foreigners. Othello is a convert to Christianity and he is a military hero, but this is not enough to give him entry into the inner citadels of Venetian society. So what does he do? He marries. He marries the fairest and most beautiful woman in Venice, Desdemona. And what does she see in him? She certainly does not marry him for looks because she says herself that she considers him ugly. Her attraction to Othello is that he tells wonderful and moving stories about faraway places and the grand exploits in which he has participated. Desdemona is a young and intelligent woman who feels restricted in the narrow, formal world of Venice. Othello represents for her a new world. But their relationship is based on a deep mutual insecurity that neither of them recognizes. The only person who recognizes this insecurity is the villain of the play, Iago. He uses it to bring about Othello's destruction.

Think about this: A man wrongly suspects his wife of adultery, kills her, and then kills himself. Allan Bloom has remarked that if this were a Greek play, it would certainly be a comedy. But there is nothing comic or ridiculous about Othello. Even though he makes horrendous errors of judgment and destroys himself, Othello is a great man. The play can be read as a tragedy of assimilation, as a profound look at the vulnerability inherent in a person who seeks to become a full member of another society. Moreover, Shakespeare's dignified portrayal of Othello, even as Iago and other characters make fun of his blackness, shows that even a work written in the sixteenth century is capable of magnificently transcending the ethnocentrism and prejudices of its time.

My conclusion is that not only do great works such as *Othello* have powerful and important things to say about prejudice and ethnocentrism—issues of special concern to minority students—but also such works demonstrate the universality of knowledge and greatness. Such universality was once the goal of leading African Americans such as scholar W. E. B. Du Bois, who envisioned a world in which "I sit with Shakespeare and he winces not. Across the color line I move arm in arm with Balzac and Dumas . . . I summon Aristotle and Aurelius and what soul I will, and they come all graciously, with no scorn nor condescension." It is in the great works of the Western tradition that minority students, and indeed all students, are most likely to discover the liberation they are seeking.

8

■ How Reagan Outsmarted the Liberals

Dear Chris,

From your e-mail, and its accompanying attachment, I see that you looked up Rigoberta Menchu on the Web and discovered that she won the Nobel Peace Prize. "Why, then," you ask, "do you portray her as such a buffoon?" My friend, you have a lot to learn about those wacky Swedes who hand out Nobel prizes. Being a buffoon is by no means a disqualification. Remember that Rigoberta won in 1992, the five-hundred-year anniversary of the Columbus landing. The Swedes were determined to show their political correctness by giving the prize to an American Indian. But who? Chief Sitting Bull was dead, and Russell Means was a bit passé. So the choice seems to have come down to Rigoberta Menchu or the actress who played Pocahontas in the Disney movie. And Rigoberta won, although thank God it wasn't for literature!

There is a further postscript to this story. In 1998, an American anthropologist, David Stoll, revealed that many of the incidents described in *I, Rigoberta Menchu* were fabricated. Stoll's allegations were checked and verified by Larry Rohter of the *New York Times*. For instance, in one of the most moving scenes in her book, Rigoberta describes how she watched her brother Nicolas die of malnutrition. But Stoll and the *New York Times* found Nicolas alive and well enough to be running a relatively prosperous homestead in a nearby town. According to Rigoberta's own family, as well as residents of her village, she also made up an account of how a second brother was burned alive by army troops as her parents were forced to watch. Central to Rigoberta's story—and the supposed source of her Marxist beliefs—is her account of how her impoverished family, working for slave wages on plantations, was oppressed by wealthy landowners of European descent. According to the locals, the dispute was really a land feud that pitted Rigoberta's father against his in-laws. "It was a family quarrel that went on for years," the mayor of the town told the *New York Times*. "I wanted peace, but none of us could get them to negotiate a settlement."

You might think that, after these revelations, Rigoberta Menchu and her book would have been cast into outer darkness. But such is the leftist mind that even facts cannot violate a morality tale! The *Chronicle of Higher Education* reported that many American professors who teach Rigoberta Menchu's autobiography intend to continue doing so, and they are angry with David Stoll for having humiliated an already-victimized woman of color. One of her American academic devotees said that even if Rigoberta did make stuff up, her memory must have been distorted by years of oppression! Personally I believe that *I, Rigoberta Menchu* has a place in the liberal arts curriculum. The book should be taught in courses that survey celebrated literary hoaxes.

Moreover, for her ingenuity in pulling off such an ingenious hoax, who can doubt that Rigoberta Menchu deserved a prize?

But enough about Rigoberta. Let us move from small things to large. Your letter makes a very interesting reference to Ronald Reagan. You remind me that you were much too young to remember Reagan as president. You grew up, poor fellow, in the Age of Clinton. Thus, instead of remembering Reagan's Challenger speech, or the signing of the Intermediate Range Nuclear Forces (INF) treaty with Mikhail Gorbachev, what you'll probably remember is your mom's turning off the television to shield your little brother from the sexually explicit parts of Clinton's impeachment hearings. No wonder you are curious about what it must have been like to grow up with a real president. "What was Reagan really like?" you want to know. "What difference did he make? How will he be remembered?" Actually, the issues you raise are discussed in my book *Ronald Reagan: How an Ordinary Man Became an Extraordinary Leader*. But I see that you are trying to save yourself $16. Very well, I will try to answer your questions.

Ronald Reagan seemed to be a very ordinary guy. He lacked all the basic credentials that our political science textbooks say are needed in a president. He was a C student at Eureka College. He spent most of his career as a movie actor. He was not a scholar or an intellectual. He had no foreign policy experience when he was first elected president. He put in a short day at the office, and allegedly took naps. He appeared to be an unserious, whimsical fellow who spent much of his time cracking jokes. To the liberal mind, and even to some conservatives, it seemed unlikely that he would prove an effective leader.

Yet even liberals know with hindsight that important things happened in the 1980s. The Soviet Union began to collapse, and socialism was discredited. Today, there are probably more Marxists on the faculty of our elite colleges than there are in all of Russia and Eastern Europe. The American economy, after being in the doldrums throughout the 1970s, went into high gear. The technological revolution really took off: Suddenly computers and cell phones were everywhere. A generation ago, John F. Kennedy told Americans who were young and idealistic to join the Peace Corps. Public service was seen as the embodiment of American idealism. But by the end of the 1980s, most young people would rather have started a new company than pick coffee in Nicaragua. The entrepreneur—not the bureaucrat—became the vehicle for youthful aspirations. This cultural shift had policy implications. The welfare state, which had expanded since the 1930s, stopped growing. The era of Big Government that began with FDR in the 1930s seemed to have come to an end in 1989, when the Berlin Wall fell. Was this not the "Reagan Revolution" that the old boy promised?

The liberals refused to believe it. Since Reagan was such a simple, dumb, sleepy, unqualified fellow, he could not possibly have directed the vast changes of the 1980s. This was the premise of Edmund Morris's official biography of Reagan, *Dutch*. Morris was selected to write about Reagan because Reagan's aides thought that a man who had written favorably about Teddy Roosevelt was bound to like Reagan. After all, TR was an outdoors guy and so was RR. What Reagan's aides ignored was that Teddy Roosevelt was also an aristocrat from an old moneyed family. And he was an intellectual who invited historians and anthropologists to the White House for learned debates on the fine points of scholarship. These are the aspects of TR that impressed Morris.

But Reagan was not like that. On several occasions, Morris visited the Reagan ranch in Santa Barbara. He probably looked on Reagan's bookshelves for the works of Thucydides and Benjamin Disraeli and Winston Churchill. They were not to be found. Instead, Morris would have seen copies of *Reader's Digest* and *Arizona Highways* and the novels of Louis L'Amour. Morris seems to have decided right then that Reagan was an unsophisticated boob. Throughout his biography, Morris beats himself over the head to figure out how such a plebian could have achieved the great things that occurred during Reagan's tenure. And ultimately Morris becomes so frustrated with solving this Reagan puzzle that he gives up, and instead of writing about Reagan he starts writing about himself. Never has a presidential biography failed so ignominiously to provide new insights into its subject. What a missed opportunity.

But let me tell you about my own experience with Reagan. I am part of a generation of young people who became interested in politics because of the Reagan Revolution. We saw Reagan as a cheerful, forward-looking guy. We loved his self-deprecating humor. Yet we also saw that, beneath that jocular exterior, Reagan was a determined man who was making some big and important claims. Indeed, he was taking on the big idea of the twentieth century, which is collectivism. Reagan wanted to halt the growth of the welfare state at home, and he wanted to dismantle the Soviet empire abroad. These were enormously ambitious goals. Many people, including most conservatives, considered Soviet Communism to be irreversible. So, too, Republicans such as Dwight Eisenhower, Richard Nixon, and Gerald Ford had made their peace with the welfare state. Reagan was the first person to say "Government is not the solution. Government is the problem."

Many of us young conservatives—including a small battalion from the *Dartmouth Review*—came to D.C. excited by Reagan and eager to be part of his revolution. In short order, many of us found ourselves working for the

Reagan administration. There was even a Dartmouth Mafia in the White House. We were able to get these jobs because Reagan didn't want to hire the old guys who had worked in the Nixon and Ford administrations. Reagan had run against Ford for the Republican nomination in 1976, and many of these guys had viciously attacked Reagan. "Who needs them?" Reagan figured. "Yes, they have experience, but it is experience in screwing up." At the age of twenty-six, I was appointed senior domestic policy analyst in the White House.

This was exciting for many reasons—big salary, big office, car and driver, the chance to make an impact on policy—but an important consideration for me was that I would finally be able to convince my family that I was doing something important. My parents had expressed concern when I chose not to attend the Wharton Business School and instead came down to Washington, D.C., to be a writer. Not only were they worried that I would starve but they weren't sure what it was that I actually did. My attempts to explain the mysterious contours of American politics were particularly ineffective. So finally I mailed my parents a photograph showing me side-by-side with Reagan. I figured that even if they still didn't know precisely what I did, they would have to reckon that it was something significant. I found out later that just as my parents opened the package, my grandmother hobbled into the room, took one horrified glance at the photograph, and then exclaimed, "What is my grandson doing with that scoundrel Richard

Nixon?" Since this incident, I have given up trying to raise the political consciousness of the D'Souza family.

The Reagan White House was an endlessly fascinating place. Walk down one hall and you'd see the Sons of Italy. On another floor a representative of the administration would be meeting with a group of Catholic nuns. Soviet émigrés with long beards sometimes showed up for a meeting with the president. On occasion, I saw Afghan children whose limbs had been blown off by Soviet mines. Every administration, I suppose, develops its own character according to the types of people it attracts. In the Clinton administration, I suspect you would have seen an entirely different crowd: union bosses, witches, transvestites, and so on.

In America, Reagan is today bathed in a warm glow of affection. Conservatives revere him, and even liberals claim to have developed a kinder, gentler feeling for the guy. This is in stark contrast to the 1980s, when liberals treated Reagan with loathing and contempt. For instance, Eric Alterman of the *Nation* described Reagan as a "pathological liar" and an "unbelievable moron" with a "heart of darkness" that showed a "fondness for genocidal murders." Normal people would be unsettled by such allegations. Think of Dan Quayle, who has labored for years to dispel the public's suspicion that he is an idiot. Reagan, by contrast, never exerted himself to rebut his critics. He even agreed with them. Once, when asked about his light work schedule, Reagan quipped, "They tell me hard work never killed anyone, but why take the chance?" During a speech at Eureka College in the mid–1980s, Reagan confronted the allegation that he had graduated from a third-rate school with a C average. Reagan mused, "Even now I wonder what I might have accomplished had I studied harder!"

Over the years, I have pondered the question of what made Reagan so successful. I have three answers. First, he had a Euclidean certainty about what he believed and where he wanted to take the country. Not only was he a man of conviction but he was a man whose convictions were not open to change. This is a key point, so let me elaborate a bit. When I was a student at Dartmouth, I was informed again and again that a liberally educated man has an open mind. Having an open mind means making only provisional judgments and always being open to new evidence that might change your mind. I realized, with some stupefaction, that Reagan did not share this view. He knew in advance what he wanted to do—say, lower taxes. If his aides informed him that the facts went in the other direction, Reagan's basic attitude was, "Okay, get me new facts."

In this, Reagan was right. In a certain sense, it is important for a president to be closed-minded. The reason is that when you are elected president and come to Washington with an agenda, you are immediately surrounded by highly competent and experienced people who tell you, "Sorry, Mr. President, but you simply cannot do that. The Congress will never go for it. There is opposition within your own party. The Supreme Court is sure to strike it down. The General Accounting Office has serious reservations. What are we going to tell the American Association of Retired People?" And so on. The open-minded person is quickly drowned in a sea of facts. Only the man with a firm rudder, only the man who has already decided where he is going is confident enough to keep going when the political waters get rough.

Second, Reagan instinctively understood that the president, powerful as he is, cannot change the world in sixty-five ways. He can change the world in only two or three ways. And so Reagan set his priorities. He wanted to defeat inflation, revive the economy, arrest the advance of the Soviet empire—and that's about it. The other stuff Reagan didn't care about. In the White House we were sometimes frustrated when Reagan avoided issues such as affirmative action and conceded to the liberals on farm subsidies and such. But Reagan understood, better than we did, that a president has to choose his fights. Early in Reagan's first term, he was criticized for failing to recognize one of his own cabinet secretaries. This was Sam Pierce, the secretary of Housing and Urban Development. Reagan saw the guy at a meeting of big-city mayors and greeted him by saying, "And how are things in your city, Mr. Mayor?" This was a bit of a gaffe, yet the reason for it was that Reagan didn't really care about the Department of Housing and Urban Development. He saw it as a rat-hole of public policy. He knew that if he went in, he might never come out. And this was probably a correct perception.

Third, and perhaps most important, Reagan was successful because he didn't care about what the elite culture said about him. Newt Gingrich and Jack Kemp are similar to Reagan in some ways, but they differ from him in that they are both anxious to win the approval of elites. As Speaker of the House, Gingrich was always troubled when he was excoriated by Dan Rather on the CBS *Evening News*. Kemp yearned for the plaudits of the editors of *Time* and the *Washington Post*. But Reagan genuinely didn't care. He had the same attitude when he was governor of California. During the late 1960s, Reagan was repeatedly attacked in the *San Francisco Chronicle* by the influential columnist Herb Caen. On one occasion, Reagan's aide, Michael Deaver, said to him, "Governor, have you seen these vicious attacks by Herb Caen?" And Reagan's response was, "Yeah. What's eating that guy?" Reagan's assumption was that something was obviously wrong with Herb Caen. He did not for an instant consider the possibility that Caen's criticisms might have some merit. This liberation from the tyranny of elite opinion gave Reagan the freedom to operate outside the bounds of what is normally permissible.

None of this is to say that Reagan refused to acknowledge any moral or intellectual authority. But his authorities were drawn from, let us say, outside the bounds of the policymaking world. The economist Arthur Laffer recalls that shortly after the U.S. invasion of Grenada in 1983, he met Reagan at a conference. He told Reagan that the newspapers had reported that the administration had gone back and forth on whether to go with the invasion. Laffer asked, "What made you finally decide to do it?" Reagan said, "Well, Art, finally I asked myself, what would John Wayne have done?" Somewhere deep down, Reagan knew that John Wayne was a better guide on this occasion than the collective wisdom of the Washington establishment.

Reagan's firm convictions and his indifference to elite opinion were responsible for the biggest and boldest decision of his presidency: the decision to cut taxes and raise defense spending even in the face of a ballooning federal deficit. The deficits not only raised the ire of Democrats but also fears within Reagan's own camp. Reagan's budget director, David Stockman, and the chairman of his Council of Economic Advisers, Martin Feldstein, called on Reagan to scale back the tax cut and moderate the defense increase. Reagan's reply was almost farcical. "Gentlemen," he said, "I believe the deficit is big enough to take care of itself." At this point, the national media went apoplectic! But Reagan was making a considered gamble. He strongly believed that the tax cuts would energize the economy, which in turn would increase the tax base and swell the revenues of the treasury. He was determined to have his defense increase to curb—and, he could only hope, topple—the "evil empire." Reagan knew that if this happened, America would be able to spend less on defense in the future. So there was a kind of logic, albeit a risky logic, behind Reagan's assertion that "if we cannot balance the budget now, we'll have to do it later."

But the Reagan gamble paid off. Although the pundits wailed for more than a decade about the Reagan deficits, the country moved into the 1990s only to discover that the annual deficit had vanished. Poof! Suddenly America was running big budget surpluses. Of course, the shameless Clinton repeatedly bowed and claimed credit for the surpluses, but what did he do to produce them? Absolutely nothing. It was the juggernaut of economic growth that began around 1983 and continued virtually uninterrupted through the 1990s that proved to be a tax bonanza for the treasury. Moreover, huge defense savings from the end of the cold war contributed to making the dreaded deficits disappear.

On the left, revisionist historians try to deny Reagan credit for his role in ending the cold war. "The Soviet Union collapsed by itself," they say. Or, "Gorbachev did it." Neither of these explanations is believable. First, the Soviet Union undoubtedly had economic problems in the 1980s, but it also had such problems in the 1970s, and the 1960s, and the 1950s. Come to think of it, the Soviets had faced economic problems ever since the Bolsheviks took power. Admittedly, these sufferings imposed continual hardships on the Soviet people, but there were no signs during the 1980s that the people were up-in-arms. No mass demonstrations, no popular revolt. Moreover, the ruling class was living comfortably, as it had since Lenin's day. So why would this group relinquish power? No empire in history has called it quits, freed its colonies, and dissolved itself just because its economy was ailing.

Nor does it make sense to say that Gorbachev brought about the change. First, Gorbachev did not want to end Communism but to save it. Gorbachev went to the Soviet military and said, in effect, Give me my economic reforms and I will have more resources for you to spend on weapons. Today, Gorbachev claims that he was always a democrat and a liberal, but go back and read Gorbachev's speeches and his book *Perestroika*, published during the 1980s. Gorbachev sought to "reform" Communism, but the system imploded because it was too rigid to adapt to the reforms. So Gorbachev was a decent bungler who ended up producing a result that he did not intend. Curiously, it was an outcome that Reagan sought and predicted when he said, in 1982, that Soviet Communism would end up on "the ash heap of history."

Another point to remember, Chris, is that Reagan was largely responsible for the Soviet Politburo's elevating Gorbachev to power. Gorbachev was completely different from the Brezhnev-Andropov-Chernenko types. So why did the Politburo choose him? The reason is that the Soviet strategy that had worked so well during the 1970s had stopped working during the 1980s. Between 1974 and 1980, ten countries fell into the Soviet orbit, starting with the fall of Vietnam and ending with the Soviet invasion of Afghanistan. After 1981, when Reagan came to power, no more real estate fell into Soviet hands; and in 1983, thanks to an American invasion, Grenada became the first country in history to be liberated from the clutches of Soviet Communism. Moreover, Reagan deployed Pershing and cruise missiles in Europe to meet the Soviet threat there. He announced the strategic missile defense program. When Chernenko died, the Politburo concluded that they needed a new type of leader to cope with this fellow Reagan. And so they put Gorbachev into the ring, where he was outmaneuvered by Reagan and ended up taking himself, and Soviet Communism, over the precipice of history.

I have emphasized left-wing revisionism about the cold war, but there is also a right-wing revisionism that focuses on Reagan's domestic policy. Some libertarians give Reagan credit for cutting taxes, but they blame him for not slashing domestic spending. Indeed, they point out, the percentage of the gross national product consumed by the federal government grew under Reagan. How could this happen? Reagan made a prudential judgment early on that he could not get his tax cuts and his defense increases through a Democratic Congress, controlled by Tip O'Neill, if at the same time he demanded substantial cutbacks in domestic spending. Reagan knew how impractical it would be for him to say, "I want billions of dollars for MX missiles and B-1 bombers, and I want to take the money out of Medicare and food stamps." Much as Reagan would have liked to see domestic cuts, he decided to leave the welfare state alone while he focused on his tax program and his foreign policy program. It is easy, with the benefit of hindsight, to second-guess Reagan about whether he could have managed some domestic reductions, but in the world of practical politics, leaders have to make hard choices about what is feasible at a given time.

The diplomat Clare Booth Luce once said that history, which has no room for clutter, remembers every president by one line only: "Washington was the father of the country." "Lincoln freed the slaves." And so on. It is interesting to speculate on how recent presidents will be remembered. So what about Reagan? Margaret Thatcher said several years ago that "Reagan won the cold war without firing a shot." This is a pretty good epitaph, but I think Reagan did more than that. So my line for him is the following: "Reagan won the cold war and revived the American economy and the American spirit." For this, all Americans owe Reagan a profound debt of gratitude.

9
▓ Why Government Is the Problem

Dear Chris,

I am delighted that you enjoyed my Reagan book so much. You cite Reagan's quip comparing the government to a baby: "It is an alimentary canal with an appetite at one end and no sense of responsibility at the other." This view, you say, is radically different from the one that prevails on your campus. The regnant ethos says, "But how can you be against government programs? The government is simply there to help people."

Yes, but which people? And with whose money? And with whose consent? And with what result?

It is one thing for the government to provide the basic necessities of life to the "truly needy," a group that would include the poor, the sick, and the disabled. It is another thing for government to take resources from one middle-class family and give them to another middle-class family. This happens when, for example, the government builds a mass transit system: People who prefer to drive cars must pay for the transportation preferences of people who prefer to take the subway. A similar redistribution is under way when the government funds the National Endowment for the Arts: Everybody has to subsidize the recreation of those Americans who want to listen to Papuan folk music, or view photographer Robert Mapplethorpe's portraits of his own genitals. I do not deny that many government programs aimed at the middle class enjoy considerable political support. As George Bernard Shaw put it, "A government that robs Peter to pay Paul can always count on Paul's support."

Many such programs corrupt our politics by making it a contest for who gets to feed at the public trough. Moreover, they do not promote the common welfare or the public good. Rather, they promote the good of some people at the expense of other people. To see why this is bad, recall the basic theory of a liberal society as articulated by early modern philosophers such as John Locke. In this view, we enter into a social contract and place ourselves under the jurisdiction of government to protect ourselves from foreign and domestic thugs, and to secure our basic rights, such as the rights to liberty and property. Why would we agree to join a society that routinely seized our resources without our consent and bestowed them on other people?

This is not to deny that the government has an important role to play. We need the government to fight terrorists and to secure the borders against illegal immigrants.

We need the government to get criminals off the street. While we can debate the means to achieve this, government can and should ensure that all Americans have access to basic education and healthcare. The government is responsible for building the highways and administering the space program. Government help is needed to protect the environment because, without such help, some companies would pollute the air and water with impunity. The government also supports basic research, provides patent protections, and establishes criteria for product safety. Conservatives should not be embarrassed to support government action in its legitimate sphere.

But at the same time, we recognize that whatever the government does, it usually does it badly. (I know of only one exception to this rule: the writing of parking tickets.) This is not to suggest that the people who work in government are less competent than those who work in the private sector. The problem is that, unlike the private sector, the government doesn't have a "bottom line." There are no clear criteria to determine whether a government program is working. Some years ago, a bureaucrat in the Washington, D.C., public school system said, "How can you say that our public school system is a failure? Lots of people work here." By his standard, the school system was impressively fulfilling its function of providing employment to lots of people.

Conservatives know that government continues to do things that aren't needed, or that could be done better by someone else. Some liberals now recognize this, too; but

I must say, they are slow learners. Frequently they must be dragged, kicking and howling, to conclusions that are patently obvious. The reason for the liberal's obstinacy and reluctance is that the miserable fellow is painfully discovering that his basic theory is wrong.

Wrong in what sense? When I was in college, I learned from my political science textbooks that the government simply must run the lighthouses, because if it didn't, no one would. I also learned that the government must deliver the mail, otherwise lots of people would never get a letter. Prisons, I was further informed, were a necessary government responsibility. Finally, my textbooks were insistent that, without public schools, millions of Americans would receive no education at all.

The experience of the past couple of decades has shown that every one of these assumptions is either dubious or demonstrably false. Today, there are many privately run lighthouses. The argument about government mail delivery has stumbled into a two-word rebuttal: Federal Express. Private mail carriers are now ubiquitous, and there is no reason to believe that they could not deliver regular mail as efficiently as they deliver packages and overnight mail. Prisons routinely contract out services to private contractors, and some prisons are entirely run by private companies. Moreover, there is no logical reason why private markets cannot provide education services through high school for all; the government's role could then be limited to providing assistance to those who would not otherwise be able to afford those services.

"But," I have heard many students ask, "Isn't Big Government necessary to check the influence of Big Business?" In a few cases—such as the recent corporate accounting scandals—the answer is yes. In general, though, the power of big business over the average American is quite limited. To sell its shares and its products, the business must persuade investors and customers. It must win their consent before taking their money.

But this is not true of Big Government. Let me illustrate with an example, which I have drawn from economist Walter Williams. The federal government has a program called Social Security that is intended to help me save for my retirement. What if I were to say, "I appreciate the gesture, folks, but no thanks. I don't want to be part of this program. I am not going to pay any Social Security taxes, and I forgo any future claim on benefits. When I am old and cannot support myself, I will draw on my private savings, or rely on relatives and friends, or appeal to private charities, and if all these measures fail I will endure my poverty." How would the government respond to this?

The government would, of course, respond by *killing me.* This may strike you as an implausible or paranoid speculation on my part, so let's explore the hypothesis further. I refuse to pay Social Security taxes. The government sends me notices and imposes fines. I ignore the notices and refuse to pay the fines. Federal agents then come to seize my property. I, taking my gun out of my desk drawer, make whatever attempts I can to protect what is mine. Since I am a poor shot and there are many more of them, the outcome can be told in advance. They will win, and I will be dead.

The purpose of this anecdote is to show that what distinguishes the government from the private sector is the power of coercion. In some ways the most insignificant government bureaucrat—the parking meter attendant, the IRS examiner, the guy at the Department of Motor Vehicles, the immigration official—has more power over me than the CEO of General Motors or General Electric. And this power of coercion, which is inherent in the nature of government, fundamentally undermines the liberal claim that the government is doing a moral thing by helping people.

Let me show you why this is so. I am walking down the street, eating a sandwich, when I am approached by a hungry man. He wants to share my sandwich. Now if I give him the sandwich, I have done a good deed, and I feel good about it. The hungry man is grateful, and even if he cannot repay me for my kindness, possibly he will try to help someone else when he has the chance. So this is a transaction that benefits the giver as well as the receiver. But see what happens when the government gets involved. The government takes my sandwich from me by force. Consequently, I am a reluctant giver. The government then bestows my sandwich upon the hungry man. Instead of showing me gratitude, however, the man feels entitled to this benefit. In other words, the involvement of the state has utterly stripped the transaction of its moral value, even though the result is exactly the same.

Now let's keep the same scenario but change the outcome. I am approached by the hungry man, as before, but this time, instead of agreeing to share my sandwich, I refuse to do so. Along comes a third man; he pulls out a gun, points it at my head, and forces me to hand over my sandwich to him, upon which he gives it to the hungry guy. What is the moral quality of the gunman's action? I think most people would consider him an unscrupulous thug who should be apprehended and punished. Yet when the government does precisely the same thing—forcibly seizing from some to give to others—the liberal insists that the government is acting in a just and moral manner. This is clearly not true.

Finally, I want to challenge the liberal notion that the private sector is motivated by greed, while the public sector is motivated by noble idealism. This is another of those liberal fictions, shamelessly peddled by Franklin Roosevelt and John F. Kennedy, and now routinely promulgated in political science textbooks. I believed it once, but only because I was ignorant. I should have asked, Why should people change their basic nature when they move from the private sector to the public sector? It was not until I worked in the White House, however, that I saw the naïveté of my presumptions.

Allow me to recount a fairly typical meeting at the White House. This one involved drug policy. The folks from the Defense Department declared that the problem was that drugs were being produced in Columbia, and they had a $20 billion program to destroy the crops. The people in the Health and Human Services Department said no, the problem of drugs was a problem of treatment, and they were in the process of developing a $40 billion program for this purpose. The Education Department's representative was convinced that the real solution to drugs was education, and his team proposed a multi-year initiative to raise the consciousness of America. Listening to these self-serving bureaucrats, I realized that, whatever the merits of their arguments, they were no less motivated by self-interest than those in the private sector. The only difference was that their self-interest was expressed in a different currency. Fundamentally, they were after power instead of money.

"The era of Big Government is over," Bill Clinton has assured us. Although the welfare state has lost some of its legitimacy, the federal government is still too large and overbearing. We should continue to limit its size, and to keep it focused on what it is supposed to do. When the state exceeds its proper functions, when it moves outside its sphere, it invades the domain of the citizens, depriving us of both freedom and responsibility.

10
▨ When the Rich Get Richer

Dear Chris,

So, you ask, does wanting to get rich make you a bad guy? Of course not. Indeed, I would go further: The rich are in the best position to be the good guys, because only the rich have the resources to really help those who are in need. Still, despite the philanthropic advantages conferred by wealth, I am not at all surprised that your roommate is outraged by your desire to make money. Your roommate apparently believes that rich people are evil because they make money and that the government is good because it takes away some of that money. Not that liberals would put it that way. They would say that the government's job is to promote equality by redistributing resources from the rich to the poor. In my last letter, I tried to argue that this attempt is wrong-headed; here, let me argue that it is unnecessary. Indeed, I intend to show that technological capitalism—not government—is the true catalyst for equality. You can consider this letter a kind of extended postscript to my previous critique of Big Government.

Whenever a Republican—be it Reagan or George W. Bush—proposes a tax cut, the liberals say, "This tax cut will mostly help the rich." *Of course* tax cuts help the rich the most; the rich in this country pay most of the taxes. I wonder how many Americans know that the top 10 percent of income earners in America pay two-thirds of all income taxes. Meanwhile, the bottom 50 percent of income earners pay less than 5 percent of the income taxes. These statistics, which I got from the Internal Revenue Service, are of obvious relevance in determining who is going to benefit most from virtually any proposal to reduce income tax rates.

Thus if the rich guy makes $250,000 and pays $100,000 in taxes, and the (relatively) poor guy makes $40,000 and pays $5,000 in taxes, a 10 percent across-the-board tax cut will cut the rich guy's taxes by $10,000 and the poor guy's taxes by $500. This provokes the liberal wail, "But the rich guy is getting twenty times more than the poor guy." One does not have to be a math major to figure out that it is not even possible to cut the poor guy's taxes by $10,000 because he pays only $5,000 in the first place. Contrary to liberal demagoguery, proportional tax cuts are just because they benefit citizens in proportion to what they have been paying in taxes.

Liberals usually oppose tax cuts and advocate higher taxes for the rich because they are convinced, as the old liberal mantra has it, that "the rich get richer while the poor get poorer." But is this really true? For the past half century, and especially for the past two decades, it has not been true in America. In reality, the rich have grown richer, and the poor have also grown richer, but not at the same pace.

Let me explain. In 1980, when Reagan was elected, America was a much more egalitarian society. According to the Census Bureau, if one earned $55,000 that year, one was in the top 5 percent of earners in the United States. That sounds amazing, but it's true. Now, taking inflation into account, $55,000 in 1980 equals something like $75,000 today. But today if you want to be in the top 5 percent of income earners, you have to make $155,000.

What this means is that lots of people who used to be in the middle class, or the lower middle class, have moved up. In moving up, they have increased the economic distance between themselves and the rest of the population. So, inequality is greater. But the exclusive liberal focus on inequality misses the larger picture, which shows that more and more people are moving into the ranks of the affluent classes.

Consider another example: millionaires. In 1980, according to the Federal Reserve Board and other government sources, there were roughly 600,000 American families with a net worth exceeding $1 million. By 1990, this number exceeded a million. Today, approximately 5 million families—made up of between 15 million and 20 million people—are worth in excess of $1 million. Indeed, the population of millionaires has swelled so much that the business magazines have redefined "rich": You now need to make a million dollars a year to qualify.

The most impressive aspect about this wealth is that it is self-created. Historically, wealth has been acquired mainly through birth or inheritance. People became rich, as the saying goes, by "choosing their parents carefully." Today in America this is not so. Most people on the *Forbes* 400 rich list didn't get there because they have rich parents; they made their own money. The authors of the best-seller *The Millionaire Next Door* estimate that 80 percent of American millionaires are entirely self-made.

My point, Chris, is that America has greatly expanded opportunity and, by doing so, has created the first mass affluent class in world history. Previously, the great economic achievement of the West was to create a middle class: to take people who were poor and give them basic comforts. The term *middle class* implies that you have adequate food and clothing and shelter, and you can afford to take an annual vacation, but you don't have wealth. This is what has changed. America has extended the privileges of affluence, traditionally restricted to the very few, to a sizable segment of its population.

The myopic liberal focus on inequality creates the false impression that the mass affluent class is a bad thing, while in fact it represents a spectacular achievement.

But what about the ordinary guy? As an immigrant to the United States, I am amazed by how well the ordinary citizen lives in this country. A half century ago, the average home size in America was 1,100 square feet; now it has doubled to around 2,200 square feet. We live in a nation where construction workers walk into coffee shops and pay $4 for a nonfat latte. Maids in America drive pretty nice cars. Take a trip on an airplane, and you are likely to find yourself sitting next to an electrician taking his third wife to St. Kitts. I have a friend in India who has been trying to move to the United States for years, but he can't seem to get a visa. Finally, I asked him, "Why are you so eager to come to America?" He replied, "Because I really want to move to a country where the poor people are fat."

I continue to be surprised by the rapid rate at which technology spreads from the affluent class to the general population. We have seen this with VCRs, with computers, with cell phones. During the 1980s, cell phones were mainly used by yuppies driving expensive cars. They were a status symbol whose social prestige derived from their relative scarcity. Today, cell phones are ubiquitous at every socioeconomic level and their status value is down to nil.

The liberal realist (admittedly a thinly populated group) may admit all this, and yet insist that technological capitalism creates scandalous levels of inequality. In the short term, this is sometimes so. In the long term, however, technological capitalism is a powerful vehicle for promoting equality. This is not widely recognized, so permit me to explain.

A hundred years ago, the rich man drove a car and the poor man walked. That was a big difference. Today, the rich man drives a new Porsche and the poor man drives a second-hand Honda Civic. That is not such a big difference. A century ago, rich families avoided the cold weather by going to Florida for the winter. Meanwhile, poor families braved the elements. Today, most families, whatever their economic status, enjoy central heating; but the poor have benefited more from this invention because it has alleviated a situation from which they previously had no escape.

Perhaps the best illustration of the egalitarian effects of techno-capitalism can be shown by life expectancy statistics. In 1900, the life expectancy in America was roughly fifty years. Rich people lived to the age of sixty, while poor people on average died at the age of forty-five. There was a fifteen-year gap in life expectancy between the rich and the poor. Today, life expectancy in America has climbed to seventy-eight years. The rich guy lives to the age of eighty, while the poor guy drops at the age of seventy-six. This is still a gap—four years—but it is vastly smaller than the fifteen-year gap of a century ago. And what has closed the gap? Advances in medicine, in nutrition, in crop yields, and so on.

My conclusion? Technological capitalism has done more to raise the general standard of living, and to equalize the circumstances of rich and poor, than all the government and philanthropic programs put together. This fact severely undermines the liberal view that aggressive government redistribution is needed to prevent growing and enduring inequality.

11
How Affirmative Action Hurts Blacks

Dear Chris,

I understand that you were burned in effigy by the Afro-American society for writing a column in the campus paper criticizing affirmative action! You lucky guy! Remember that the people who reacted so strongly have serious doubts that they belong at your university. By raising the issue publicly you have aroused black shame, which camouflages itself as black indignation.

How should you respond to this? Write another column! The activists' slogans and angry e-mails should be enough to get you started. I have been reading through the e-mails, which you forwarded to me, and some of the issues they raise call for a serious response. I have written this letter to help address some of these issues. I have gone beyond the activists' complaints, however, and framed the discussion in a question-and-answer format.

What is affirmative action? Affirmative action was originally defended as a means to assure the genuine equality of opportunity. Its advocates usually presented it as a special effort to recruit more minority applicants. The presumption was that affirmative action would be a form of outreach, that minority applicants would be held to the same standard as nonminority applicants, and that the program would be temporary. How differently things have turned out. In practice, affirmative action means adopting racial preferences. It means giving preference in university admissions, job hiring, promotions, and government contracts to less qualified black and Hispanic applicants over more qualified white and Asian American candidates. Many advocates of affirmative action say that preferences should end only when prejudice and discrimination come to an end; in short, they want such programs to continue forever.

Don't women also benefit from affirmative action? In many cases, yes. Many colleges have eliminated preferences for women in admissions because women are now the majority on most campuses, even on campuses that used to be all male. But women still benefit from gender preferences in jobs, promotions, and government contracts. Some defenders of affirmative action like to point out that "white women as a group benefit most from preferential policies." If this is true, it is an excellent reason to get rid of affirmative action. These policies were originally aimed at benefiting one group only: African Americans. Blacks were held to have suffered unique and special hardships: slavery, state-sponsored segregation, Jim Crow, lynching, and so on. The earliest affirmative action measures were restricted to blacks. But then other groups—women, Hispanics, and so on—came along and insisted, "We are victims of discrimination, too." And at first the black leaders were incredulous. "No way," they said, "Were you folks ever enslaved? Lynched? Forced to drink out of separate water fountains?" But then a second camp within the civil rights movement spoke up. Their point was that, as a minority, blacks would be forever dependent on white goodwill to maintain affirmative action preferences. "But if we include Hispanics, who are nearly 10 percent, and women, who are 50 percent of the population, we can keep these programs going for as long as we want." This second group prevailed, and ultimately other groups were allowed onto the bandwagon, not because they had a moral case, but to strengthen the political coalition to maintain these preferences indefinitely.

Don't affirmative action policies fight discrimination? No. Consider two virtually identical scenarios. A white guy and a black guy apply for a position. The black guy is better qualified; the white guy gets the position. That's racial discrimination. Here is the second scenario. A white guy and a black guy apply for a position. The white guy is better qualified; the black guy gets the position. That's affirmative action. Now, in what sense is the second result a remedy for the first? It is not. All I see are *two instances* of racial discrimination.

Isn't discrimination a problem in college admissions? No. I do not deny that discrimination by universities is an historical reality. It used to be a problem. But not any longer. Where are the bigots in the admissions offices who are keeping blacks and Hispanics out? Such bigotry is not even alleged. Let me go further, Chris: There is no evidence to show that black or Hispanic students who have been preferentially admitted over the past few decades have been victims of discrimination. Moreover, there is no evidence to show that white or Asian American students who have been turned away—despite having stronger grades, test scores, and extracurricular talents—have discriminated against anyone.

What about charges that the standardized tests are racially biased? This charge is completely false. Consider the math section of the test. A typical question goes like this: "If a train can go 90 miles in an hour, how far can it go in 40 minutes?" No one can argue with a straight face that equations are racially biased, or that algebra is rigged against Hispanics. Yet the same gap in performance between racial groups that we see on the verbal section of the test is also present on the math section. Numerous studies have confirmed that the test accurately measures differences in academic skills.

Do these standardized tests predict college performance? Yes. Tests are in the business of prediction. No test can predict future performance with complete accuracy. Standardized tests, however, have repeatedly been shown to be the best predictors of college performance.

The reason is pretty obvious when you consider the alternative criteria used by admissions officers. Recommendations are essentially meaningless. "Not since Jesus Christ has there been a person who has shown such potential to change the course of history as young Wilbur." Grades depend entirely on where you went to high school. Most high school teachers grade on a curve. So a 3.8 grade average from a mediocre school may not mean as much as a 3.4 grade average from a really good school. The great benefit of a standardized test is that everyone takes the same test, therefore it is possible to compare students' performances on one scale.

Don't colleges give preference to athletes and alumni children? Yes, but athletic ability is a talent. It is part of the broad package of abilities that colleges can and should consider in admitting students. Virtually no institutions admit applicants on academic merit alone. If you are a champion violinist, if you have studied yoga in the Himalayas, if you do community service—these things count in your favor. So why should admissions officers not take into consideration your talents as a good quarterback or an outstanding lacrosse player? Alumni preferences are much harder to justify. They are basically a fundraising mechanism: The alumni are a major source of funding, and one way that colleges maintain their continuing allegiance is by admitting their children and grandchildren. When this issue came up in a recent debate, I said to my opponent, "I agree with you that alumni preferences are unfair. So why don't we join together in condemning both alumni preferences and racial preferences?" At this suggestion, he became very nervous and refused my invitation. I realized that he wasn't really against alumni preferences; his point was that since nepotism is already in place, why not allow minority applicants to benefit from it? In a rapid turnaround, our civil rights leaders have gone from attacking nepotism and embracing merit, which was the Martin Luther King approach, to embracing nepotism and attacking merit, which is the Jesse Jackson approach.

Isn't it a problem when minorities are under-represented at selective colleges? That depends on what is causing the under-representation. Consider the example from the National Basketball Association. African Americans represent 12 percent of the population, yet more than 75 percent of professional NBA players are black. Is this a problem? Why aren't people demanding to see more Jews and Koreans on the courts? The reason is that people recognize that merit is producing the disparate outcome. If teams pick the best passers, dribblers, and shooters, then it doesn't really matter that one group is over-represented and other groups are under-represented because merit, not discrimination, determines the result. Similarly, if a larger percentage of white and Asian American students are getting into Berkeley on merit, that is a result we should be willing to live with.

Why not raise the floor for under-represented groups? Because college admissions is a zero-sum game. Every seat that is given to a black or Hispanic student with weaker qualifications must be taken away from an Asian American or white student with stronger qualifications. In short, there is no way to raise the floor without lowering the ceiling. It's an algebraic impossibility. Therefore, much as we'd like to see more black and Hispanic faces at top schools, this result should not be achieved by unjustly rejecting better-qualified Asian Americans and whites.

Can't you support any form of affirmative action? In my previous work I have written in favor of affirmative action based not on race but on socioeconomic status. If a student who comes from a disadvantaged background and goes to a lousy school nevertheless scores in the 90th percentile on the SAT, he or she may have more college potential than another student who comes from a privileged background and scores in the 95th percentile. So colleges can and should take socioeconomic circumstances into account. Remember, too, that more blacks and Hispanics would be eligible for socioeconomic affirmative action, since blacks and Hispanics disproportionately come from the ranks of the poor.

How does affirmative action hurt blacks? African Americans face two serious problems in America today. The first is "rumors of inferiority." Many people don't like Koreans or Pakistanis, but hardly anyone considers these people inferior. With blacks, however, there remains a widespread suspicion that they might be intellectually inferior. Far from dispelling this suspicion, affirmative action strengthens it. Affirmative action conveys the message to society that "this group is incapable of making it on its own merits." Racial preferences are a sort of Special Olympics for African Americans. Such preferences devalue black achievement, and they intensify doubts about black capacity.

The second problem facing African Americans is cultural breakdown: high crime rates, broken families, illegitimacy, and so on. These cultural problems are in my view the main reasons blacks do poorly on many measures of academic achievement and economic performance. The way to improve black performance is to address this cultural breakdown. Racial preferences are a distraction from this challenge. They create the illusion that blacks are performing poorly due to racism. By rigging the race in favor of blacks, affirmative action policies prevent African Americans, and society in general, from doing the hard and necessary work of building African American cultural skills so that blacks can compete effectively with whites and other groups.

If affirmative action hurts blacks, why do blacks support it? The reason is that affirmative action provides short-term gains. Imagine the situation of a liberal who approaches me and says, "Dinesh, you are a victim of hundreds of years of British imperialism. I am going to pay you $3,000 a month to compensate for this historical crime." Now imagine that the liberal's offer is challenged by a conservative who says to me, "Dinesh, don't take the money. You don't really need it. You have had a good education and can compete on your own merits. Also, the subsidy may prove to be a disincentive for you to become self-reliant." I would thank the conservative for his troubles and take the liberal's money!

What about the success stories of affirmative action? They do exist. I recently spoke at Deerfield Academy, where a black student said to me, "I didn't have the academic credentials to get into Deerfield. I was admitted on a special program for minority students. But now I have an A-grade average. I am vice president of my class. I am on the track team. Am I not a success story of affirmative action?" I told him, "Yes, you are. But here you are at one of the best prep schools in the country. Do you want another preference to get into Princeton? And another one to get into Yale Law School? And another one to get a job? And another one to get a promotion? And another one to get a government contract? That's not right, my friend. You have been given a break and you have taken advantage of it; now you should be willing to compete on your own merits, and may the force be with you."

1 2
■ The Feminist Mistake

Dear Chris,

You say in your letter that you are more worried about the feminists than about the black activists. I am not, for the reason given several years ago by, of all people, Gerald Ford. Ford said there would never be a war between the sexes because there is too much fraternizing with the enemy. Gender conflict simply does not pose the same dangers of social balkanization that are produced by racial conflict. Let me try, nevertheless, to meet your request and give you an account of what's wrong with modern feminism.

The feminists at elite universities are, by and large, an angry bunch. This seems odd, because they are paid very well and are living very well. These feminists communicate their anger in very nice lounges over expensive meals and fancy cocktails. Their "martini rage" is directed against such things as "institutional discrimination." Why aren't more women teaching math and physics? Why aren't more female thinkers being assigned in the philosophy and literature departments? Why do women earn seventy cents for each dollar earned by men?

The answer to these questions is obvious, yet one is not supposed to say it. Let me give the answer obliquely by turning to a writer whom feminists greatly admire. In her book *A Room of One's Own*, Virginia Woolf raised a provocative question: Why is there no female Shakespeare? What if Shakespeare had had a sister, Woolf speculates, would she have become a writer and won the same fame as her brother William? Woolf answers that there is no female Shakespeare because women have historically not been given rooms of their own—that is to say, the opportunities and resources and leisure—in which to write.

Woolf may have provided a satisfactory explanation for the absence of a female Shakespeare, but underlying this explanation is a hard truth: There is no female Shakespeare! This means that literature courses, if they are based on merit, are going to be heavily weighted toward male authors. And what is true of literature is even more true of philosophy and science.

What about the earnings discrepancy? The seventy cents figure that feminists have publicized is accurate enough, but it carries the presumption that women are earning 70 percent of what men earn for doing the same job. In fact, this is not true. Where is the evidence that the U.S. government or U.S. companies systematically pay men more than women to perform identical jobs? It does not exist. The statistic means that on average women earn less than men. But should we be surprised that female executive assistants make less money than male executives? Reasons for the male-female earnings difference could be that women choose different fields than men, that women sometimes drop out of the work-force to raise children, and so on.

But there is another factor that could help to explain why, at the most advanced levels of academic and economic performance, men tend to do better than women. This factor is intelligence. I am not suggesting that men have higher IQs than women. On the contrary: Countless studies have shown that men and women have the same average IQ of 100. Upon closer examination, however, we see that IQ is distributed differently among women than among men.

Male and female IQ can be plotted on a bell curve. The mean score for the two groups is the same, but the bell curves look different. The female bell curve is taller and narrower; the male bell curve is shorter and flatter. This means that female performance tends to congregate around the mean, whereas among men, there are many more geniuses—and many more dummies. I believe this finding is confirmed by experience. Men tend to win the literature prizes and the Westinghouse Science Awards, but men are also over-represented among the truly dumb. When I walk into a social gathering, I am pretty sure that the most exceptional person there is going to be a man and that the biggest idiot there is also going to be a man.

Another indication of male over-representation at the lower end of the bell curve can be seen in crime rates. A large body of research shows that criminals are, in general, very dumb people. Not surprisingly, the vast majority of criminals are men. Incidentally, John Gotti, the Mafia don, was tested at school and had an IQ of 109. How, then, did he become the most powerful figure in the Mafia? Because an IQ of 109 puts him in the genius category for the criminal class!

All this brings me to the feminist mistake. Women and men once had separate domains. The female domain was the private world of home and family, and the male domain was the public world of work and politics. Each world had its own value, and the two could not be rightly compared; indeed, in some respects the female world could be considered more consequential. As one male wag said to his wife, "You decide what we eat for dinner, which church we attend, and where we go for vacation, and what our children should study, and I decide whether we are for Mr. Dewey or Mr. Truman."

Then something happened that pushed women into the male sphere, and career women aspired to compete effectively with men for the most lucrative rewards of the male sphere. According to feminists, the large-scale movement of women into the workforce was the consequence of the great feminist revolution that stormed the barricades of the patriarchy and won a glorious victory, although the battle is ongoing. This is a lovely fairy tale, but when exactly did the battle occur? How many people were killed? Why did the entrenched patriarchy put up so little resistance?

Let us put aside buncombe and talk a little sense. Technology, not feminism, paved the way for mass female entry into the workforce. The vacuum cleaner, the forklift, and the birth-control pill had far more to do with this than all the writings of Betty Friedan and all the press releases put out by the National Organization for Women. Think about this: Until a few decades ago, housework was a full-time occupation. Cooking alone took several hours. The vacuum cleaner, the microwave oven, and the dishwasher changed that. Until recently, work outside the home was harsh and physically demanding. Forklifts and other machinery have reduced the need for human muscle. Finally, before the invention of the pill, women could not effectively control their reproduction and therefore, for most women, the question of having a full-time career simply did not arise.

So technology made it possible for women to work. This was perhaps inevitable, but what was not inevitable was the shift of values that went with the change. The feminist error was to embrace the value of the workplace as greater than the value of the home. Feminism has endorsed the public sphere as inherently more constitutive of women's worth than the private sphere. Feminists have established as their criterion of success and self-worth an equal representation with men at the top of the career ladder. The consequence of this feminist scale of values is a terrible and unjust devaluation of women who work at home. This has been recognized. Less noticed has been the other equally unfair outcome: Women are now competing with men in a domain where, at the very top level, they are likely to lose.

13
Who Are the Postmodernists?

Dear Chris,

I am not sure that it was the wisest idea to share my letter on feminism with the chairwoman of the Women's Studies department. Isn't this the woman who looks like Janet Reno, wears ridiculous hats, and comes to class with a big dog? She sounds quite terrifying. Now if I am found in a back alley mauled by a bloodhound or stabbed in the back with a hatpin, you will know where to direct the authorities.

You note that much of the humanities program—including the Women's Studies department—is made up of "postmodernists." Who, you ask, are the postmodernists? The postmodernists are the Truly Profound Ones. By way of illustration, let me offer this passage by literary theorist Geoffrey Hartman. "Because of the equivocal nature of language, even identities or homophones sound on: the sound of Sa is knotted with that of ca, as if the text were signaling its intention to bring Hegel, Saussure, and Freud together. Ca corresponds to the Freudian Id ('Es'); and it may be that our only 'savior absolu' is that of a ca structured like the Sa-significant: a bacchic or Lacanian 'primal process' where only signifier-signifying signifiers exist."

This has all the hallmarks of postmodern thought. It is pompous, verbose, and incoherent. To a certain type of intellectually insecure person, postmodernism and its intellectual cousin, deconstructionism, can appear profound: "Gee, that sounds very complicated. These people must be incredibly brilliant." Tens of thousands of graduate students have been fooled in this way by people such as Hartman and the master of postmodernism, Jacques Derrida. Serious thinkers see through Derrida in an instant. Michel Foucault reportedly said of Derrida, "He's the kind of philosopher who gives bullshit a bad name."

It would be a mistake, however, to dismiss all postmodern thought in this way. Philosopher Richard Rorty and literary critic Stanley Fish are both lucid writers, and they put forward substantial claims. Their fundamental claim is that there is no such thing as objective truth. Even science, Rorty and Fish assert, does not describe "the world out there"; rather, it is a Western cultural construction that has no more claim to reality than anyone else's cultural construction. In an article in the *New York Times*, Fish even suggested that the rules of science are just as arbitrary as the rules of baseball.

Postmodern theory suffers from the weakness that the postmodernists themselves don't believe it, as their actions show. When Richard Rorty needs a medical checkup, he doesn't go to a witch doctor; he checks into the medical center at the University of Virginia. When Stanley Fish and I debate on campus, we do not travel there in an oxcart; we go by plane. "Show me a relativist at 30,000 feet," Richard Dawkins writes, "and I'll show you a hypocrite." Airplanes fly, Dawkins points out, because a lot of Western mathematicians and engineers "have got their sums right."

In other words, science works because the universe operates according to certain regularities or laws, and science is devoted to discovering those laws. Of course, scientists do not claim knowledge of final or objective truths, but they do insist that the Newtonian account of the universe is superior to the Ptolemaic account, and that the Newtonian account has itself been surpassed by that of Albert Einstein. Even though scientific hypotheses may be culturally conditioned, it is only when they have survived criticism and testing that they are held to be valid and true.

Too embarrassed to challenge the authority of science, some liberal scholars concede that facts are known, but they insist that values are relative. These scholars are, strictly speaking, logical positivists rather than postmodernists, and their view appears much more reasonable. After all, we can verify facts but values would seem to be the product of individual and cultural preferences.

The Greeks, however, thought otherwise. The ancient Greeks held that there was a moral order in the universe that was no less real or true than the laws governing the motions of the planets. Moreover, the Greeks believed that this moral order was accessible to human reason, much like the laws of nature. On what basis do liberal scholars reject the Greek view? They point to the existence of widespread moral diversity. People in America disagree about morality, and different cultures have different views of morality. Thus the prevalence of moral disagreement is offered as evidence that there is no moral truth.

But the liberal view is not convincing. So what if people disagree about values? People also disagree about facts. If the Gallup organization conducted a survey of the world's people and the world's various cultures, it is quite possible that most people and most groups would emphatically reject Einstein's proposition that $E=mc^2$. This disagreement would hardly refute Einstein; it would prove only that the majority of the world's people are wrong. So, too, the presence of moral disagreement proves nothing about whether moral truths exist. Socrates argued that, if anything, disagreements invite investigation so that we can determine which moral opinions are true and which are false.

In my view, the great intellectual challenge facing conservatives is to make the case for morality at a time when many in the West have ceased to believe in an external moral order. The decline of belief in such an order is the most important political development of the past two centuries. Indeed, this decline has created the "crisis of the West." This crisis is not simply one of the "death of God." Rather, as Friedrich Nietzsche predicted, if religion withers away, so does morality. The reason is that religion is the primary source of morality, and therefore morality cannot long survive the decay of religion.

What is the liberal response to this decline of morality? To welcome it, in the name of freedom. That was Nietzsche's response as well. Liberals, like Nietzsche, speak about creating "new values." Some liberals even dream about creating a "new man" free from the traditional impediments of human nature. The liberal commune, based on shared possessions and free love, is one such social experiment. The Nazis and the Communists also tried to create new men and new values, with less benign results.

Conservatives recognize that efforts to change human nature and invent new values are both foolish and dangerous. Conservatives accept human nature for what it is, and are cautious about schemes to alter it. Moreover, conservatives prefer to stand by old values while recognizing that they need to be adapted to new circumstances. Our challenge, different from that of conservatives in the past, is to articulate reasons for those values to a society that has lost its moral consensus.

14
■ Why Professors Are So Left-Wing

Dear Chris,

The postmodernists may be an especially loony bunch, but their prominence in the academy raises the question: Why are professors so left-wing? Each year the *Chronicle of Higher Education* publishes a survey of the attitudes of professors, including their political identification. Liberals outnumber conservatives by more than two-to-one, and the ratios are even greater in the humanities and social sciences. Moreover, this ratio becomes more lopsided as one moves to more selective and elite universities. What's going on here? Writer Michael Kinsley has an explanation: Professors are simply more intelligent than the rest of the population. If this is true, it poses a problem for conservatives. Do education and intelligence lead one to adopt the liberal viewpoint?

Hardly. There are many intelligent conservatives, but they tend to be in business. Conservatives tend to go into business because they care more about money; liberals tend to go into the academy because they care more about power. One reason for this divergence of interests is that conservatives in general are practical people—they emphasize what works—while liberals are theoretical people—they emphasize what ought to work. "Why do people have to work for gain? Why can't they work out of solidarity with the community?" When you hear someone talk like this, you know you are listening to a liberal.

This is not to say that conservatives have no interest in becoming professors. Some do, but they are usually concentrated in economics or the hard sciences. Once again, the reason has to do with the conservative bent toward practicality: equations that add up, theories that can be tested, and so on. By contrast, liberals prefer such fields as sociology and literary criticism because in these areas their theoretical perspective never has to meet the test of reality.

I am probably not typical of conservatives in that I once seriously considered becoming a professor of history, literature, or American studies. But, as I realized soon after graduating from Dartmouth, a grim future awaited me in the field of American studies. The place is a mecca for radicals. "Truth in advertising" demands that it be called un-American studies. The point is that once liberal ideologues dominate a field or a department, they frequently conspire to keep conservatives out.

Consider Harvard's black studies program. Its spectrum of opinions ranges from liberal to radical-left.

There are no conservatives in the department. Is this because there are no conservative academics good enough for Harvard? Not at all. Thomas Sowell at the Hoover Institution has arguably produced more original work than half of Harvard's black studies department. Some of the liberals at Harvard are utterly mediocre figures who would be teaching at community colleges if they weren't liberal and they weren't black. Sowell, too, is an African American, but he is the wrong kind of African American. Despite his prodigious scholarship, he falls outside the range of acceptable opinion in those quarters.

So part of the reason for the liberal bias in academia—especially in the humanities and social sciences—is that the academy reflects a temperamental and ideological self-selection at work. But there is a second reason why professors, as a group, tend to be liberal. They have a visceral hostility to capitalism, one of the reasons why so many once found themselves attracted to Marxism (and some are still). Not that they find Marx's theories about surplus value or his predictions about the future to be particularly convincing. They turn to Marxism as a vehicle for expressing their animus toward capitalism.

Why, then, do professors dislike capitalism? Because they are firmly convinced that capitalist societies are unjust. Many professors believe that, in a just society, the largest share of wealth and influence should be held by the most intelligent people, that is to say, *themselves*. In a capitalist society, by contrast, the ones who have the most influence and make the most money are entrepreneurs. The typical Ivy League professor may earn $100,000 annually, but he is outraged to see a fat Rotarian with a gold chain dangling on his chest pulling in $1.5 million a year selling laundry detergent. He concludes that something has to be wrong with a world that produces results like these.

That's when he becomes a registered member of the Democratic Party.

15
■ All the News That Fits

Dear Chris,

If there is one institution that is even more left-wing than the typical American university, it is the media. Most reporters, I realize, deny this obvious fact. They cannot deny that journalists overwhelmingly vote for Democratic candidates and support liberal causes because several surveys have documented this. What they do deny, therefore, is that their personal convictions have anything to do with their reporting.

But is it possible to stand in isolation from one's deeply held views when one is covering stories that have political significance? Some reporters don't even bother. These fierce ideologues are few, but they are sometimes found in influential places. A few years ago, Fox Butterfield wrote an article about conservatism in the *New York Times* in which he quoted me as saying, "The question is not whether women should be educated at Dartmouth.

The question is whether women should be educated at all."

I called up Butterfield and informed him that while that line had appeared in the *Dartmouth Review*, its author was another student, Keeney Jones. I said that I would appreciate Butterfield's publishing a correction. Butterfield became defensive. He pointed out that I had *quoted* the line in question in one of my *Policy Review* articles. "So you did say it," Butterfield insisted. I was dumbfounded. I told Butterfield that, by his logic, *he* could now be held accountable for the line since he, too, had quoted it in *his* article. The man still didn't get the point, and he refused to correct his error. Now, we are not talking about some dimwit but about a Pulitzer Prize–winning journalist at a leading newspaper.

I cannot believe that this kind of extreme bias is typical. Probably most journalists aspire to objectivity. Some even recognize that they hold liberal convictions and work hard in their stories to include alternative points of view. Usually, however, journalists allow their ideological compasses to shape their work without even realizing it. During the 1980s, many reporters couldn't bring themselves to call the Sandinistas "Marxists" even though that's what the Sandinistas called themselves. Instead, they called the Sandinistas "left-leaning," as if they were the Latin American equivalents of Tom Daschle. Today, journalists routinely call John Ashcroft "ultraconservative," but they don't call Ted Kennedy "ultraliberal." From their point of view, Ted Kennedy is basically a centrist because he occupies the same position on the political spectrum that they do.

Media bias is a big problem because many Americans open the newspaper or turn on the television set and they think they are witnessing "the news," that is, what just happened. They don't seem to realize that countless things have occurred, and that a crucial process of selection determines what they read and see. What gets into the newspaper, what goes on page 1, what the headline says, which picture is chosen to illustrate the article, which premises shape the way the article is written—these are all subjective decisions made by editors and writers. And they are highly susceptible to ideological manipulation.

Most Americans don't realize that behind the news stories they read are what may be termed "meta stories." The meta story is the hidden general premise that controls the specific news story. During the 1980s, the "meta story" shaping news coverage was that Reagan's economic policies were having disastrous social effects. One such effect, according to the media, was homelessness. That's why we saw countless articles and television features on "the homeless." Homelessness was identified as a major problem. Millions of people were said to be homeless. Then, suddenly, homelessness ceased to be a social problem. This change corresponded with the election of President Clinton. During the Clinton era there were hardly any stories on the subject. Had all those people found homes? Of course not. But most journalists did not identify Clinton's policies with hurting the poor. They lost interest in the homeless because the homeless had ceased to illustrate the follies of Reaganism.

What are some of the other "meta stories"? One is "Another Vietnam." Every time the United States intervenes abroad—whether in Grenada or Bosnia or Afghanistan—a chorus of voices in the media warns that it's Vietnam all over again. Terms such as "bogged down" and "quagmire" start surfacing in *Newsweek* and the *Boston Globe*. Dan Rather's expression becomes even more constipated than usual. Never mind how often the Vietnam analogy is proved wrong: It is embedded in the psyche of a media generation that came of age during the Vietnam era. Another "meta story" is Women and Minorities Hardest Hit. You've probably seen the headline: "The Bush Economic Program: Women and Minorities Hardest Hit." Columnist Joseph Sobran notes that, if nuclear war erupts, the headline in the *New York Times* will read, "Nuclear War Breaks Out: Women and Minorities Hardest Hit."

These "meta stories" are generally immune to refutation. As an illustration I submit a series of articles that appeared recently in the *New York Times*. The premise of these articles was that it was highly ironic and troubling that more Americans were in prison than ever before at a time when violent crime rates were shrinking. It never seemed to occur to the editors that maybe violent crime rates were shrinking *because* many of the criminals were locked up!

Unlike many conservatives, who are incensed by media bias, I take a wry view of it because I think that it is becoming less of problem. First, more and more Americans realize that Peter Jennings and Tom Brokaw don't just report the news; they are instrumental in deciding what is news. The *New York Times* doesn't present "all the news that's fit to print" but "all the news that fits." This is not to say that the *Times* isn't worth reading. It is a valuable expression of the Manhattan liberal Jewish perspective. Once people figure out the ideological compass that is directing their news they become more critical viewers and readers.

A second reason for optimism is that the liberal monopoly on the way the news is reported has been effectively shattered. *Time* magazine, the *New York Times*, and the major television networks once had a shaping influence on virtually all the major news stories, from Watergate to the Iran-contra hearings. Those days, thank God, are over. Now lots of people get their information from talk radio and from the Internet and from cable news channels such as Fox News. Suddenly there is real diversity in what Americans see and hear. The liberal pundits fret about the decline of American journalism—Americans prefer the Fox News Channel to PBS! People would rather listen to Rush Limbaugh than to Bill Moyers!

But journalism isn't in decline, only liberalism. Americans prefer Limbaugh, Matt Drudge, and the fiery faces on the Fox News Channel because they are in the *Dartmouth Review* mold: jocular, outrageous, and unafraid to slaughter sacred cows. Not only are these right-wing figures more interesting, they are also more insightful than liberal drones such as Moyers. Not only are the liberal drones consistently wrong, they are sanctimoniously convinced that they are right and that they are better than everyone else. They have been done in by that little device called the remote control because now Americans have alternatives. It's great, and there's nothing that the liberals can do about it.

16
■ A Living Constitution?

Dear Chris,

Having said what I think about liberal professors and about liberal journalists, I will now tell you my view of liberal judges. This group is probably the most corrupt of all, corrupt not in the sense of taking bribes, but in the sense of betraying the basic function of a judge. Yes, the very concept of the "liberal judge" is an oxymoron, and the presence of so many liberal judges in our courts has had the most deleterious consequences for our society and for our system of government.

We have witnessed nothing less than a social revolution in America in the past half century. This social revolution was not produced by the American people. It was produced by the Supreme Court, and then imposed on the American people. "But we are not undermining the democratic process," the liberal advocates of these changes insist. "The judges are merely interpreting the Constitution."

Well. The Constitution is indeed our supreme law, and it is the function of the Supreme Court to interpret the law. But liberal judges have gone beyond interpretation in making rulings that fundamentally revise the Constitution. The liberals have effectively rewritten the Constitution in a manner that those who wrote that document would not recognize. Moreover, liberal scholars such as Laurence Tribe and Bruce Ackerman have produced a theory of jurisprudence that says the Constitution is a living document and that judges should feel free to adapt it as they see fit to current circumstances.

Let's begin by looking at what the Supreme Court has done. Without any constitutional authority, it has invalidated numerous state laws on such matters as school prayer and the regulation of obscenity. But, the liberal will say, what about the specific constitutional provision of "separation of church and state"? What about the First Amendment? Actually, there is *no* specific constitutional provision for the separation of church and state. Moreover, the First Amendment clearly specifies, "Congress shall make no law . . ." It is a restriction on federal, not state, power.

Liberal judges Earl Warren, William Brennan, and Thurgood Marshall devoted their careers to trying to take things that they don't like out of the Constitution, such as gun rights and the death penalty, while putting in things that conform to their liberal ideology, such as constitutional protections for abortion, homosexual rights, and obscenity. Today this addition and subtraction process continues with judges Ruth Bader Ginsburg, Stephen Breyer, and David Souter. In a sense, these people are policymakers masquerading as judges.

If that seems an unduly harsh way of putting it, let me try to show why it is duly harsh. Consider the "right to privacy" that the Supreme Court invoked in striking down all state laws that restricted abortion. Where is this right to be found in the Constitution? The document contains specific privacy protections, such as the right against "unreasonable search and seizure." But there is no general right to privacy. Examine the text, hold it up to the light, read it backwards in the mirror— it just isn't there. *Roe v. Wade,* the 1973 decision declaring abortion a constitutional right and invalidating numerous state laws regulating abortion, represented a grotesque abuse of judicial authority. Yet even today the Supreme Court continues to uphold, and even expand, this "right."

Let me be clear: I am not here debating the policy merits of the Supreme Court's decisions about school prayer, obscenity, and abortion. Possibly the liberals are right that public prayer is dangerous and that perusing obscene materials and killing the unborn have great social merit. Personally, I would question such priorities, but I am not interested in doing so here. Here I am simply raising the question of whether these are policy issues that it is the role of the Supreme Court to decide.

Does the Constitution confer legitimate warrant for the Court to settle such questions?

In a famous speech a few years ago, Justice William Brennan answered yes: "For the genius of the Constitution rests not in any static meaning it might have had in a world that is dead and gone, but in the adaptability of its great principles to cope with current problems and current needs." This sounds reasonable, but it should take only a moment's reflection to see why it is utterly bogus. Sure, the Constitution needs to adapt and change, but the framers anticipated this. There is a procedure specified in the Constitution—the amendment process—by which the document can be changed. And several times during the course of American history the Constitution has been amended. But it takes an overwhelming majority in the Congress and in the state legislatures—a virtual consensus of the society—to do this. The framers wisely made it hard to change the Constitution so that it would remain an expression of the enduring will of the people and not become the property of any particular interest group.

By exploiting the discretion that is inherent in the process of interpretation, the liberals have succeeded in hijacking the Constitution for their own political ends. In essence, liberals frequently seek to use the courts to bring about political and social changes that they cannot achieve by amending the Constitution or by going through the democratic process. One target of contemporary liberal judicial activism is the death penalty. The Constitution specifically provides for the death penalty.

A sizeable majority of Americans support it. It is unlikely bordering on impossible for liberals to amend the Constitution to impose a comprehensive ban on the death penalty. But liberal judges are seeking to use the "equal protection" and "cruel and unusual punishment" clauses of the Constitution to strike down the death penalty.

Once again, I am not here debating the merits of the death penalty. There is a legitimate argument over whether the death penalty effectively deters violent crime, although my personal observation is that not one of the criminals who have been executed over the years has ever killed again. However this may be, the issue here is whether judges should have the power to make a ruling that specifically contravenes the Constitution and also goes against the wishes of the American people. Here the liberals generally say yes, and the conservatives generally say no.

The question goes to the heart of what kind of society we are. In a democratic society, the people make the laws. The judge's job is to interpret the law, to apply it to specific cases. When judges go beyond their constitutional authority in making laws they usurp the prerogatives of the legislature and of the people. Do we want to be ruled by nine unelected individuals drawn from a relatively narrow segment of society, or do we want to be ruled by people elected in the manner that the Constitution provides?

The role of the judge is like the role of an umpire in a baseball game. The umpire does not make the rules. The rules are given to him. His job is to apply the rules. The fairness of the game depends on whether the umpire performs this neutral function. The liberals, however, want their judges not to be umpires but to be players. They want activist judges who will issue rulings that are congruent with liberal ideology.

The liberal success in this area poses a special problem for conservatives. For years conservatives have advocated a jurisprudence of "judicial restraint." Let us have judges, President Bush says, who will issue rulings that are within the parameters of the Constitution. In theory this makes sense, but in practice it is not enough for conservatives to seek judges who are restrained, who refrain from imposing their personal views on their rulings. If liberal judges push left and conservative judges remain neutral, the result will be a continual ratcheting toward the left. This is what has happened over the past half century.

What is needed, therefore, is a couple of decades of right-wing judicial activism.

Conservative judges should give the liberals a dose of their own medicine. One exciting possibility is to invalidate the provisions of the progressive income tax by finding them inconsistent with the equal protection clause of the Fourteenth Amendment. Who cares that the Fourteenth Amendment was intended to address entirely different issues? Who cares that its provisions were intended to apply to the states?

When the liberals scream, they should be solemnly assured that the Constitution is a living document, we should not be constrained by old rules, we now understand better how multiple levels of taxation create multiple classes of citizens, and so on. The goal here is to teach the liberals a lesson, to show them that two can play at this game. Let us hope that, by demonstrating how judicial activism can be invoked to harm the causes they hold dear, we can persuade the liberals to adopt the view that judges should interpret laws and not make them.

17
More Guns, Less Crime

Dear Chris,

I was amused to read about the safety briefing that you attended on campus following the attack on a female student in her sorority house. The campus police, you say, counseled students to engage in "passive resistance" if confronted by a criminal. Now it is true that, when an unarmed person is confronted by an armed criminal, passive resistance is generally better than fighting back. But that's because "fighting back" involves everything from using one's fist to kicking and screaming to trying to run away. "Fighting back" doesn't work for female victims because their assailants are almost always men, and men are typically much stronger than women. By far the safest way to defend oneself against criminal threat is to own a gun and know how to use it.

That guns deter crime is well known to many liberals, especially those politicians and celebrities who make the loudest public noises in favor of gun control. Take Richard Daley, the mayor of Chicago, or any number of Hollywood bigwigs. These people routinely assert that there is no advantage to owning guns. Yet many of them have full-time bodyguards who follow them everywhere they go. What hypocrites these liberals are! Mayor Daley wouldn't even consider setting foot in some of the crime-infested neighborhoods of Chicago without his gun-toting bodyguards. But the people who live in those areas, mostly the poor, face continuing danger, and yet Mayor Daley does not want them to to protect themselves with guns.

But what about the police? Isn't it their job to protect people? Yes, but you know as well as I do, Chris, that the typical campus police officer is far more adept at reaching for his doughnut than for his gun. Moreover, how often are the police on the scene when a crime is being committed? Usually the police show up after the fact and then try to track down the criminal. The best protection for a person who is being attacked is not to yell for the police, who are too far away to help, but to reach for a concealed weapon. Indeed, since many crimes are never solved, the police department may even be a lesser deterrent to criminals than the knowledge that an intended victim may be carrying a gun.

These speculations have been given empirical support by Yale economist John Lott, whose study *More Guns, Less Crime* is the largest ever conducted on the effects of gun control laws. After examining every county in the nation over two decades, Lott and his colleagues found that the more restrictive the gun control laws in a given county, the higher its crime rates! In general, when counties pass right-to-carry laws, which allow people of sound mind who have no criminal record to carry guns, their crime rates go down. Moreover, when counties make it more difficult for their law-abiding citizens to buy and carry guns, their crime rates go up. The reason for these outcomes is not merely that gun-owners are in a position to defend themselves against criminals, but also that criminals are more likely to be deterred when they don't know who is armed and who is not.

But what about "sensible" gun laws that require background checks, mandatory waiting periods, safety locks, and that guns be kept hidden and out of the reach of children? Lott shows that background checks are largely useless since they have no effect in preventing criminals from acquiring guns. Mandatory waiting periods mainly extend the period in which people are vulnerable to crime before they can secure the protection of a firearm. You may be surprised to discover, Chris, that the number of young children who die by setting off a firearm is very small: between thirty and fifty a year. Of course, even one death is tragic, but vastly more children drown in pools and bathtubs, or are killed in automobile accidents, than die from self-inflicted gun wounds. Yes, gun owners should keep their guns under lock and key, out of the reach of children, but guns also have to be accessible for use when needed.

None of this is to deny that guns are dangerous things, like automobiles. Recklessness with guns, as with cars, can lead to accidents and suffering. We do need gun laws, and the National Rifle Association supports laws that prohibit the possession of guns by convicted violent criminals, laws forbidding the sale of guns to juveniles, and laws requiring computerized criminal records checks on retail gun purchases. Gun owners also need to be educated, and no organization provides better or more comprehensive education than the NRA.

But the single-minded liberal focus on the dangers of guns can blind us from seeing that guns, like cars, also make our lives better and more secure. Guns do this by making it easier for us to defend ourselves. For women, guns are a great equalizer: They neutralize the strength advantage that male assailants enjoy. For people who live in dangerous neighborhoods or who engage in dangerous professions—like operating a grocery store, or driving a cab—guns are a virtual necessity.

Upon completing his research, John Lott, a mild-mannered Yale professor, went out and bought a 9 mm Ruger. If these criminal attacks persist on your campus, Chris, my advice to you is take a study break and go out and get yourself a gun.

18

How to Harpoon a Liberal

Dear Chris,

I really enjoyed the details of the "gun debate" you had with your history professor. When he began to quiver and describe your views as "truly scary"—that, Chris, was when you could feel sure you had really gotten to him. One way to be effective as a conservative is to figure out what annoys and disturbs liberals the most, and then keep doing it.

Yes, harpooning liberals is a lot of fun. I am especially fortunate because I get paid to do it. I lecture to college groups and to business groups. The business groups pay me better and treat me better. Their conferences are usually at very nice resorts, and there is typically a limousine to pick me up. By contrast, college towns are often in the middle of nowhere, the food and accommodations are mediocre, and sometimes there is no one to meet me at the airport, so I end up telephoning my student contact in his dorm.

Even so, I continue to do college lectures for two reasons. The first is that I enjoy them. My speaking is an equivalent of college teaching but without having to grade papers and deal with irascible department chairs and administrators with room-temperature IQs. I get to speak to large groups of students who, even if they disagree with me, have come voluntarily to hear what I have to say. I have also had the pleasure of debating a wide range of characters: Jesse Jackson; Kweisi Mfume, head of the NAACP; Nadine Strossen, head of the ACLU; Mary Francis Berry, head of the U.S. Civil Rights Commission; and leading liberal scholars such as Cornel West and Michael Eric Dyson. My series of debates with Stanley Fish even led to that rarest of outcomes, a genuine friendship.

A second reason I do so many college lectures is because they are desperately needed. Our campuses have become intellectually quite monolithic. Recently, a student came up to me and said, "Until I heard your lecture, my liberal arts education had not really begun, because my basic assumptions remained unquestioned." More typically, students come up to me and say, "Wow, that was really interesting. I've never heard this stuff before." And they're being truthful: They haven't. The central arguments that underlie the great debates about globalization, the role of America, the impact of new technologies, and the issue of cultural decline are utterly unfamiliar to students on our best campuses. How tragic.

Liberals love to talk about diversity and to celebrate diversity, but when they get a real dose of it, they often react with horror. I discovered this more than a decade ago when *Illiberal Education* was published. I vividly recall a talk I gave at Tufts University, where I was alarmed to see a group of students sitting in the front row *in chains*. These students, who were African American males, had chained themselves to each other, and to their seats. I guess their point was that my criticisms of affirmative action amounted to a justification of oppression. Even before I started my lecture, the students noisily rattled their chains. I was inexperienced in handling protesters at the time and I didn't know how I could possibly give my talk with all the noise. Nor was anyone from the administration in sight to establish any kind of order.

Fortunately, I was saved by divine intervention. The controversy over my appearance had brought out a huge crowd, and students were crowding the hallways and standing outside. So the organizers decided to move the lecture to a larger hall. As the crowd shifted to the new location, the protesters were still chained to their seats! "Where's the key?" one fellow yelled out.

Since then I have become quite a veteran at handling dissent. While I relish speaking and debating at left-wing campuses—some people consider it my specialty—I am less enthusiastic about speaking at campuses that are left-wing and lowbrow. I am thinking of campuses such as San Jose State or the University of South Florida. On these campuses, a large contingent is both radical and dumb, a lethal combination. These students listen to the facts I present; but because they are too uninformed and inarticulate to rebut them, they experience an inner rage. More than once, I have had a student run shrieking from the room. Sometimes the students simply cover their ears, or shout out obscenities. In a way I sympathize with them: Their worldview has come crashing down, and it is very painful for them to cope with this recognition.

At more highbrow campuses, the students don't react in this way. Sometimes, just as I begin my speech, a student sitting in the front row will slowly and deliberately stand up, stretch out as if in an uncontrollable yawn, and then pick up his backpack and slowly walk out, obviously drawing the attention of everyone in the audience. This is a situation in which, as a speaker, I have to humiliate the student completely if I am to defeat his distraction strategy and regain the audience's attention. There are several ways to do this. Usually, I address the student, "Excuse me." He turns around; he doesn't expect me to do this. And then I say something like, "It's the third door on the right." And then, as if explaining the situation to the audience, "I realize that diarrhea can be a serious problem." There is a burst of laughter, the focus of the audience returns to me, and now I can go on with my speech.

Hecklers can be intimidating, but the speaker has a great advantage: He has the microphone. Not long ago, while I was lecturing at UCLA, an American Indian whose body was literally a billboard of buttons began to shout. Every time I said something, no matter how benign, he would yell, "That sounds like Hitler." "That's just what Hitler thought." "More Adolf Hitler." Finally I had to pause and say, "Look, if you keep this up, by the end of this talk you will have given Hitler a good name." That shut him up.

The brighter students don't go the route of the heckler. They try to outsmart the speaker. "Mr. D'Souza, I appreciate your quotation from Orlando Patterson, but you have quoted him out of context." To this I reply, "Of course I have quoted him out of context. *All* quotations are out of context. If I were to quote him in context, I would have to quote his entire book." Another condescending opener that I have heard several times is: "Mr. D'Souza, has it occurred to you . . ." What follows is a question that I have heard a hundred times before. "Mr. D'Souza, has it occurred to you that you are a beneficiary of affirmative action? How, then, can you criticize it?" When I hear a question like this, I rub my chin, as if thinking deeply, before giving my ready answer. "I may have benefited from affirmative action. I didn't ask for it, but I may have received it. If I have, then my reaction is not to be pleased but ashamed. The reason is that it puts all my accomplishments into question. No matter what I achieve in life, there will always be someone to snicker and say: Well, yes, but he only got there through affirmative action. And, look, it isn't some Ku Klux Klan guy saying that, it's liberals like you! So the premise of your question illustrates one of the ways in which racial preferences harm those of us who are minorities."

On more than one occasion I have been asked, "You have made some interesting points, but isn't it true that you can only say these things because you are not white?" The person asking this expects me to go into stuttering denial. Instead, I say, "Of course that is true. As a person of color I enjoy a kind of ethnic immunity, and that allows me to speak with much greater candor. If a white guy said the things that I say, he would be hounded off the podium! This shows the degree to which the race debate is rigged. Many people's opinions are excluded at the outset. My goal, therefore, is to use my ethnic immunity to raise the curtain on some of these taboo issues, and to expand the parameters of what it is permissible to say, so that we can have an honest discussion that includes all parties."

Some questions are so inane that I find it hard to believe that I am in a university setting. Indeed, the caliber of questions I have heard from professors over the years confirms my suspicion that many people in the academy are educated beyond their intelligence. Recently, I heard the following challenge from a law professor at Texas Tech: "Mr. D'Souza, I was appalled by your simplistic remarks. Your comparison of the United States and other cultures was completely tautological. You should have compared America to its own ideals."

I replied, "Professor, let me begin by noting your misuse of the term *tautological*. If I say 'all bachelors are single,' that would be tautological, because the term 'bachelor' means one who is single. My comparison of America with other cultures may be an inappropriate analogy, but it most definitely isn't tautological."

This was very embarrassing for the professor, so he attempted a salvage operation. "You are not answering my question!" he cried out.

"I am about to answer your question," I said, "but first I wanted to expose something that is underlying your question, which is pseudo-sophistication." This was a crusher. The audience laughed and applauded, and I could see that even the professor's radical supporters were wearing pained expressions.

One tactic that I have lately encountered on campus comes from students and professors who stand up and say to me, "How can you say that racism has declined? I am white, and I am a racist." When I first heard this, from a young white professor of education, I was dumbfounded. My amazement increased when the black students in the audience began to applaud the self-confessed racist. Then I realized why: Here was a white person corroborating the black students' belief that America is a racist society. How, I asked myself, should I respond to this weird self-incrimination? I decided to take an aggressive approach. "Well, you say that you are a racist and this is probably true. I am glad that you recognize it, and that you want to make amends for it. So why don't you resign from this university and make room for a black or a Hispanic person?

Why not give up *your* seat?" When the professor expressed reluctance, I continued, "Why are you hesitating? Come on, why not put some action behind your convictions? You remind me of the humorist who said during the Civil War, 'I have already given two cousins to the war, and I stand ready to sacrifice my wife's brother!' In supporting racial preferences, you are happy to sacrifice other people's careers to pay for your misdeeds."

This was enough to answer the young education professor, but on another campus an elderly sociologist who had also proclaimed himself a racist continued the argument this way: "But giving up my seat would be *too easy*," the cunning rogue said. "I want to stay at this university so that I can fight for affirmative action and for other forms of social justice. That is the best way for me to make amends."

"Let us imagine," I said, "that you have stolen furniture from someone else's house. You are in possession of stolen goods. Now the victim comes to you and says, 'I want my furniture back.' You refuse. The victim says, 'But it's my furniture.' You answer, 'But for me to give it back would be too easy. I am going to keep the furniture. But at the same time I intend to fight harder than ever for laws against theft.' Wouldn't this be a ludicrous position to take?"

And so it goes. I am trying to give you a flavor for what these arguments sound like.

What, then, is my objective? It is threefold: to inspire and invigorate the conservative students, who often feel besieged; to flummox and bewilder the radical students, who are for the most part immune to persuasion; and to persuade the students in the political middle, who are the majority on most campuses. If I can achieve these three goals, then my labors on the campus are fully justified.

19

■ Lies My Teacher Taught Me

Dear Chris,

I have just completed a series of lectures at an elite preparatory school in the Northeast. This is a feeder school for Ivy League colleges and for places such as Stanford, the University of Chicago, and so on. While the students of these prep schools tend to be more open-minded and less jaded than those at elite colleges, there is evidence that the great liberal propaganda machine has already started to work on them. I saw that these teenagers are routinely assigned books that present a partial, tendentious, and even flatly wrong picture of America—and specifically of the American founding. Since I'm on deadline to complete a book review for the *Weekly Standard*, I'll limit myself to a couple of examples.

"The Constitution was a racist document," one student informed me. "After all, it says that a black person is three-fifths of a human being." When I asked the student his source he showed me his textbook, and there it was. But the charge is totally false. The notorious three-fifths clause of the Constitution reflects no denial of the equal worth of African Americans. Indeed, it has nothing to say about the intrinsic worth of any group. The clause arose in the context of a debate between the northern states and the southern states over the issue of political representation.

The pro-slavery South wanted to count blacks as whole persons to increase its political power. The North wanted blacks to count as nothing, not for the purpose of rejecting their humanity, but to preserve and strengthen the antislavery majority in Congress. It was a Northerner, James Wilson of Pennsylvania, who proposed the three-fifths compromise.

The effect of the compromise was to limit the South's political representation and thus its ability to protect slavery. Frederick Douglass, the great black abolitionist, understood this. He praised the three-fifths clause as "a downright disability laid upon the slaveholding states" that deprived them of "two-fifths of their natural basis of representation." So the notion that the three-fifths clause demonstrates the racism of the American Constitution is both wrong and unfair.

Another textbook accused the American founders of being plagiarists. I learned about this from a teacher who told me that he no longer respected the framers: "They stole their ideas from the Iroquois Indians."

I expressed surprise. "You mean," I said, "that free elections, separation of powers, checks and balances, and freedom of speech and religion were all invented and practiced by the Iroquois?"

"Absolutely," he said. And then, in a condescending tone, "Maybe it's time you went home and did your homework."

Well, I have done my homework, and here is what I found. There was indeed an Iroquois League that had been formed to adjudicate disputes among warring Indian tribes. Sometimes the group's efforts at mediation failed, but in general the league was reasonably successful in keeping the peace.

Benjamin Franklin heard about the Iroquois League, and in 1754 he wrote a letter to some associates in Philadelphia. Here is the essence what he said: If a bunch of "ignorant savages" can peacefully settle their differences, surely we civilized men should be able to agree upon a Constitution! And this is pretty much the extent of the connection between the Iroquois and the American founding.

I could give you other examples of ideological distortion, Chris, but I need to sign off in order to write my *Weekly Standard* review of Lester Thurow's latest. Thurow's book contains so many whoppers that I feel a bit like the mosquito at the nudist colony—I don't know where to begin.

20

■ Was Lincoln a Bad Guy?

Dear Chris,

I am glad you enjoyed the Accuracy in Academia conference that I recommended to you. You express surprise, however, because several speakers were critical of Abraham Lincoln. "Wasn't he a Republican?" you ask. Yes, indeed. He has also been traditionally regarded, both by historians and by the American people, as the nation's greatest president. But in recent years powerful movements have gathered—on both the political right and left—to condemn Lincoln as a flawed and even wicked man.

For both camps, the debunking of Lincoln usually begins with an exposé of the "Lincoln myth." This myth is well described in William Lee Miller's recent book *Lincoln's Virtues.* How odd it is, Miller writes, that an "unschooled" politician "from the raw frontier villages of Illinois and Indiana" could become such a great president. "He was the myth made real," Miller writes, "rising from an actual Kentucky cabin made of actual Kentucky logs all the way to the actual White House."

Lincoln's critics have done us all a service by showing that the actual author of the myth is Abraham Lincoln himself! It is Lincoln who, over the years, carefully crafted the public image of himself as Log Cabin Lincoln, Honest Abe, and all the rest of it. Asked to describe his early life, Lincoln answered with reference to Thomas Gray's poem *Elegy Written in a Country Churchyard:* "The short and simple annals of the poor." Lincoln disclaimed great aspirations for himself, noting that if people did not vote for him, he would return to obscurity, being used to disappointments.

These pieties are inconsistent with what Lincoln's law partner, William Herndon, said about him: "His ambition was a little engine that knew no rest." To be sure, in the ancient world, ambition was often viewed as a great vice. In Shakespeare's *Julius Caesar*, Brutus gives as his reason for joining the conspiracy against Caesar his fear that Caesar had grown too ambitious. But as James Madison notes in *The Federalist*, the American system was consciously designed to attract ambitious men. Indeed, ambition was presumed natural to a politician and favorable to democracy as long as it sought personal distinction by promoting the public good through constitutional means.

What unites the right-wing and left-wing attacks on Lincoln is that they deny that Lincoln respected the law and that he was concerned with the welfare of all. The right-wing school—made up largely of Southerners and some libertarians—holds that Lincoln was a self-serving tyrant who rode roughshod over civil liberties, greatly expanded the size of the federal government, and ultimately destroyed half the country to serve his Caesarian ambitions. In an influential essay, the late Mel Bradford excoriated Lincoln as a fanatic who, determined to enforce his Manichean vision of good and evil on the country as a whole, ended up corrupting American politics and thus left a "lasting and terrible impact on the nation's destiny."

Although Bradford viewed Lincoln as a kind of manic abolitionist, many in the neo-Confederate camp deny that the slavery issue was central to the Civil War. Rather, they insist, the war was driven primarily by economic motives. Essentially, the industrial North wanted to destroy the economic base of the South. Charles Adams, in a recent book *When in the Course of Human Events: Arguing the Case for Southern Secession*, contends that the causes leading up to the Civil War had virtually nothing to do with slavery!

This neo-Confederate attempt to rewrite history has been going on for more than a century. Alexander Stephens, the former vice president of the Confederacy, published a two-volume history of the Civil War between 1868 and 1870 in which he hardly mentioned slavery and insisted that the war was an attempt to preserve constitutional government from the tyranny of the majority. But this is not what Stephens himself said in the great debates leading up to the war. In his Cornerstone speech, delivered in March 1861, when the South was in the process of seceding, Stephens argued that the American Revolution had been based on a premise that was "fundamentally wrong." What was that premise? "The assumption of the equality of the races." Stephens insisted that, by contrast, "Our new government is founded upon exactly the opposite idea. Its foundations are laid, its cornerstone rests upon the great truth that the Negro is not equal to the white man. Slavery—subordination to the superior race—is his natural and normal condition. This, our new government, is the first, in the history of the world, based upon this great and moral truth."

This speech is conspicuously absent from neo-Confederate revisionist history. And so are the countless affirmations of black inferiority and the "positive good" of slavery—from Senator John C. Calhoun's attacks on the Declaration of Independence to Senator James H. Hammond's insistence that "the rock of Gibraltar does not stand so firm on its basis as our slave system." It is true, of course, that many whites that fought on the Southern side in the Civil War did not own slaves. But, as Calhoun himself pointed out in one of his speeches, they, too, derived an important benefit from slavery. "With us the two great divisions of society are not the rich and the poor, but white and black; and all the former, the poor as well as the rich, belong to the upper class, and are respected and treated as equals." Calhoun's point is that the South had conferred on all whites a kind of aristocracy of birth, so that even the most wretched and degenerate white man was determined in advance to be better and more socially elevated than the most intelligent and capable black man. That's why the poor whites fought—to protect that privilege.

But what about Lincoln? Contrary to Mel Bradford's high-pitched accusations, Lincoln approached the issue of slavery with prudence and moderation. This is not to say that he waffled on the morality of slavery. "You think slavery is *right*, and ought to be extended," Lincoln wrote Alexander Stephens on the eve of the war, "while we think it is *wrong*, and ought to be restricted." As Lincoln clearly asserts, it was not his intention to get rid of slavery from the Southern states. Lincoln conceded that the American founders had agreed to tolerate slavery in the Southern states, and he confessed that he had no wish, and no power, to interfere with it there. The only issue—and it was an issue on which Lincoln would not bend—was whether the federal government could restrict slavery in the new territories. This was the issue of the presidential campaign of 1860; this was the issue that determined secession and war.

But didn't the South have a right to secede? Lincoln's argument is that the Southern states entered the Union as the result of a permanent compact with the Northern states. The Union was based on the principle of majority rule, with constitutional rights carefully delineated for the minority. Lincoln insisted that since he had been legitimately elected and had taken no action to violate any constitutional provision, the Southern decision to secede amounted to nothing more than the right of any group to leave the country when it did not like the results of a presidential election. No constitutional democracy could function under such an absurd rule. Of course, the Southerners objected that they should not be forced to live under a regime that they considered tyrannical; but Lincoln countered that a decision to dissolve the original compact could occur only with the consent of all the parties involved. Once again, it makes no sense to have agreements when one of the parties can unilaterally withdraw and go its own way.

I find Lincoln's argument completely convincing on these points, and the rest of the libertarian and neo-Confederate case against Lincoln to be equally without merit. Yes, Lincoln suspended habeas corpus and arrested Southern sympathizers, but let us remember that the nation was in a desperate war in which its very survival was at stake. Of course, the federal government expanded during the Civil War, just as it expanded during the Revolutionary war, and during World War II. Governments need to be strong to fight wars. But where is the evidence for the neo-Confederate insistence that Lincoln was the real founder of the welfare state? The welfare state came to America in the twentieth century. Franklin Roosevelt should be credited, or blamed, for that. He institutionalized it, and Lyndon Johnson and

Richard Nixon expanded it. It is both foolish and anachronistic to blame Big Government on Abraham Lincoln.

Now let me say a word about the left-wing attack on Lincoln. This group of critics, composed of liberal scholars and African American activists, is harshly critical of Lincoln on the grounds that he was a racist who didn't really care about ending slavery. The indictment against Lincoln is as follows: He didn't oppose slavery outright, only the extension of it; he said (in his letter to Horace Greeley) that if he could save the Union without freeing a single slave he would do it; he opposed laws permitting intermarriage, and even opposed social and political equality between the races. If the neo-Confederates disdain Lincoln for being too aggressively antislavery, the left-wingers scorn him for not being antislavery enough. Both groups, however, agree that Lincoln was a self-promoting hypocrite who said one thing while doing another.

Some of Lincoln's defenders have sought to vindicate him from these attacks by contending that he was a "man of his time." This will not do, because there were several persons of that time, notably the Grimke sisters and Charles Sumner of Massachusetts, who forthrightly and unambiguously attacked slavery and called for its immediate and complete abolition. In one of his speeches, Sumner said that while there are many issues on which political men can and should compromise, slavery is not one of them. "This will not admit of compromise. To be wrong on this is to be wholly wrong. It is our duty to defend freedom, unreservedly, and careless of the consequences."

Careless of the consequences. Here we have that recognizable thing, the voice of Lincoln's contemporary liberal critics who (whether they know it or not) are the philosophical descendants of Sumner. One cannot understand Lincoln without understanding why he agreed with Sumner's goals while consistently opposing the strategy of the abolitionists. The abolitionists, Lincoln saw, were not primarily concerned with restricting or ending slavery. They were most concerned with self-righteous moral display. They wanted to be in the right and—as Sumner himself says—damn the consequences! In Lincoln's view, abolition was a noble sentiment, but abolitionist tactics, such as burning the Constitution and advocating violence, actually promoted the cause of slavery.

Let us answer the liberal critics by showing them why Lincoln's understanding of slavery—and his strategy for defeating it—was superior to that of Sumner and his modern-day followers. Lincoln knew that the statesman, unlike the moralist, cannot be content with making the case against slavery. He must find a way to carry out his principles to the degree that circumstances permit. The key to understanding Lincoln is that he always found the meeting point between what was right in theory and what could be achieved in practice. He always sought the common denominator between what was good to do and what the people would go along with. In a democratic society, this is the only legitimate way of advancing a moral agenda.

Consider the consummate skill with which Lincoln deflected the prejudices of his supporters without yielding to them. During the debates in Illinois with Stephen Douglas in the race for the Senate, Douglas repeatedly accused Lincoln of believing that blacks and whites were intellectually equal, of endorsing full political rights for blacks, and of supporting "amalgamation," or intermarriage, between the races. If these charges could be sustained, if enough people believed them to be true, then Lincoln's career was over. Even in the free state of Illinois—as throughout the North— there was widespread opposition to full political and social equality for blacks.

So how did Lincoln handle this difficult situation? He used a series of artfully conditional responses. "Certainly the Negro is not our equal in color—perhaps not in many other respects; still, in the right to put into his mouth the bread that his own hands have earned, he is the equal of every other man. In pointing out that more has been given to you, you cannot be justified in taking away the little which has been given to him. If God gave him but little, that little let him enjoy." Notice how little Lincoln concedes to prevailing prejudice. Lincoln never acknowledges black inferiority; he merely concedes the possibility. And the thrust of his argument is that even if blacks are inferior, this is no warrant for taking away their rights.

Or again, facing the charge of racial amalgamation, Lincoln says, "I protest against that counterfeit logic which concludes that because I do not want a black woman for a slave, I must necessarily want her for a wife." Lincoln is not saying that he wants, or does not want, a black woman for his wife. He is neither supporting nor opposing racial intermarriage. He is simply saying that from his antislavery position it does not follow that he endorses racial amalgamation. Elsewhere, Lincoln turned antiblack prejudices against Douglas by saying that slavery was the institution that had produced the greatest racial intermixing and the largest number of mulattos.

Lincoln was exercising the same prudent statesmanship when he wrote his famous letter to Horace Greeley asserting that his main objective was to save the Union and not to free the slaves. Lincoln wrote this letter on August 22, 1862, a year and a half after the Civil War broke out, when the South was gaining momentum and the outcome was far from certain. From the time of secession, Lincoln was desperately eager to prevent border states—Maryland, Delaware, Kentucky, and Missouri—from seceding. These states had slavery, and Lincoln knew that if the issue of the war was cast as an issue over slavery, his chances of keeping the border states in the Union were slim. And if all the border states seceded, Lincoln was convinced (and rightly so) that the cause of the Union was lost. Moreover, Lincoln was acutely aware that the many people in the North who were vehemently antiblack saw themselves as fighting to save their country rather than to free slaves. Lincoln framed his case against the Confederacy as one of saving the Union so that he could maintain his coalition—a coalition whose victory was essential to the cause of antislavery. And ultimately it was because of Lincoln that slavery came to an end. This is why the neo-Confederates can never forgive him.

There is more to say about Lincoln, but this letter has gone longer than I intended. Not only do I admire Lincoln, I love the guy. To me, he was the true "philosophical statesman," one who was truly good and truly wise. Standing in front of his critics, Lincoln is a colossus, and all the Lilliputian arrows hurled at him bounce harmlessly to the ground. I confess that I cannot put Ronald Reagan—not even George Washington—in the same category as Lincoln. He is simply the greatest practitioner of democratic statesmanship that America and the world have yet produced.

21
■ The Self-Esteem Hoax

Dear Chris,

I understand that the president of your college has proposed "self-esteem workshops" for women and minorities. The premise of this seems to be that racism and discrimination cause these groups to feel bad about themselves, and that this low self-image translates into women avoiding "hard" fields, such as engineering, and into blacks and Hispanics doing poorly in school. If only we raise the self-esteem of these groups, the reasoning goes, surely the women will enroll in engineering courses in greater numbers and the blacks and Hispanics will produce higher test scores. Such reasoning is fallacious.

Is it important to feel good about yourself? I am not sure about this. Sometimes when I feel very good about myself, I am on my guard because I realize that I am about to do something incredibly stupid. Feeling good about myself does not make me smarter or better. Alas, these truths are lost on modern liberals.

One reason liberals support political correctness is that they believe stern social controls are needed to prevent insensitivity and bigotry because those things gravely injure the self-esteem of women and minorities. So, too, many liberals don't like standardized tests because some people do better on those tests than others, and liberals worry that poorly performing students may suffer blows to their self-esteem. One school program, Outcomes Based Education, downplays grades and other measures of merit and instead focuses on such things as maintaining "emotional and social well-being" or developing "a positive personal self-concept."

In addition, liberals frequently seek to modify the traditional curriculum in colleges and universities because they assume that reading Plato, Dante, and John Locke reinforces the self-esteem of whites while undermining the self-esteem of minorities. The general assumption here is that white students have big smiles on their faces because, you know, Homer wrote the *Iliad*. Liberals want the curriculum to emphasize the achievement of non-Western cultures and minority groups. In a sense, they are attempting to reassure minority students by saying, in effect, "Are you down in the dumps? Don't worry, your ancestors invented the traffic light."

Self-esteem is a very American concept and Americans, perhaps more than anyone else in the world, tend to believe that feeling good about yourself is an essential prerequisite to performing to the best of your ability. Self-esteem is also a democratic idea. In a hierarchical society, one's self-image is determined by one's designated role: as brahmin, as elder, as patriarch, as peasant, and so on. Aristocratic societies do not speak of self-esteem but of honor. In a democratic society, self-esteem is claimed as an entitlement. Unlike honor, it does not have to be earned. Self-esteem in the West is largely a product of the romantic movement, which exalts feelings over reason, the subjective over the objective. Self-esteem is based on the wisdom that Polonius imparts to Laertes: "To thine own self be true."

But does a stronger self-esteem make students learn better? This seems dubious. Institutions such as the Jesuits and the U.S. Marines have for generations produced impressive intellectual and motivational results by *undermining* the self-esteem of recruits. I am the product of a Jesuit education, and one of my Jesuit teachers liked to say that "be yourself" is absolutely the worst counsel you can give some people. He's right: This is not the kind of advice we want to give to Charles Manson or Hitler. The Jesuits and the marines are both famous for first degrading the pride and self-image of youngsters and then seeking to reconstruct them on a new and firmer foundation.

Several years ago, a group called the California Task Force to Promote Self-Esteem (no, I am not making this up) conducted a study to explore the relationship between self-esteem and academic performance. The study found, to its own evident chagrin, that higher self-esteem does not produce better intellectual performance. Nor does it produce more desirable social outcomes, such as lower teen pregnancy or reduced delinquency.

These findings have been corroborated by academic studies—footnoted in my book *The End of Racism*—comparing the self-image and academic performance of American students with that of students from other industrialized countries. Consistently, American students score higher on self-esteem. Yet on actual reading and math tests, American students perform near the bottom. These results show that it is possible to have a healthy ego and be ignorant at the same time. Similarly, within the United States, black males have (you may be surprised to discover) the *highest* self-esteem of any group. Yet on academic measures black males score the lowest. The reason is that self-esteem in these students is generated by factors unrelated to studies, such as the ability to beat up other students or a high estimation of one's sexual prowess.

None of this is to suggest that the research on self-esteem shows no relationship between self-confidence and academic performance. There is a relationship, but it runs in the opposite direction. Self-esteem doesn't produce enhanced achievement, but achievement produces enhanced self-esteem. In other words, feeling good about myself doesn't make me smarter. But when I study hard, when I discover the meaning of a poem, when I find the amoeba under the microscope, when I see my way through a difficult math problem, then I feel exhilarated, and my self-esteem is justly strengthened.

That's a lesson that I wish more liberal educators would take to heart.

22
■ Who Cares About
the Snail Darter?

Dear Chris,

As you say in your letter, liberals think that conservatives don't care about the environment. But this is silly. We like trees, rivers, and baby seals as much as the next guy. Indeed, as conservatives, we should be dedicated to conserving God's green earth, and we are. It is hard to quarrel with the environmentalist claim that the ecosystem is a precious and fragile thing, and that man has the power to destroy it. The stewardship of nature is now a human responsibility.

The problem with the environmentalists is that the movement seems to have been taken over by the enviro-nuts: vegetarians, organic farmers, fruit-juice drinkers, garbage-sorters, tree-huggers, and earth-worshippers. These people do not have a reputation for being rational. Indeed, they seem to operate in perpetual alarmist mode. Thus they routinely exaggerate the threat that economic growth, technology, and human beings themselves pose to the planet. Moreover, the solution of many environmentalists—to restrict growth, to oppose "artificial" technologies such as pesticides and bioengineering, and to limit the aspirations of the world's people—is impractical and harmful. Recycling and organic farming are not the answer.

Let's begin with the tall tales that environmentalists Lester Brown and Paul Erlich have been spinning for decades. They have warned that the earth is running out of food and water, that pollution levels never abate, that the population of the earth is surpassing the earth's capacity, and that massive ecological and human disasters are imminent. In reality, agricultural production per head has risen; known reserves of fossil fuels and most metals are greater than previously thought; economic growth has produced lower birth rates and successful efforts to reduce pollution levels, and none of the horrors predicted by the environmentalists has come to pass.

Global warming? I confess that I am not agitated by it. Scientists estimate that the earth's temperature has risen by one or two degrees over the past one hundred years. I repeat: over the past one hundred years. This is a problem? One of the drawbacks of life in the United States is that it's too cold! If global warming is causing a rise of two degrees per century, by my calculation the United States will have the perfect temperature in the year 2700 A.D. True, by this time the people along the Equator may have to put on quite a bit of sunscreen, but Brazil's loss is Minnesota's gain.

On a more serious note, Chris, I believe that the solutions of the environmentalists are even less plausible than their forecasts. How likely is it that the environmentalists can persuade people in the West, and in the Third World, to limit their aspirations to have a better life? How convincing is it to say to a Brazilian farmer, "We are more concerned about the rain forest than about your chances to feed your family?" Does it make sense to tell a poor logger, "Don't cut down those trees because they are home to a very rare breed of ant?" There is virtually no chance for such arguments to succeed. Nor are the environmentalists likely to convince Third World people to have fewer children because the world is projected to have too many people in the year 2050.

The basic flaw of the environmentalist approach is its unremitting hostility to growth, affluence, and technology. Indeed, growth, affluence, and technology are the best hopes for saving the earth. Rich people—not poor people—join the Sierra Club. Only when countries become rich do they start worrying about pollution, and have the resources to tackle the problem. Moreover, affluence is a nation's best contraceptive: It is a universal demographic law that when countries become wealthier, their birth rates drop. Indeed, the wealthiest nations have seen birth rates drop so low that they are considerably below replacement levels.

Finally, technology—not the naturalistic lifestyle—is the best way to preserve the environment. Organic farming, for instance, provides employment for lots of poor, simple folk and produces crops that upper-middle-class people are willing to pay more for. Organic farming, however, is inefficient. It consumes large tracts of land to produce very small potatoes and strawberries. High-yield farming is vastly more efficient. Pesticides and bioengineering help farmers produce the most crops out of the least amount of land. When we get higher yields from our farms, we leave more room for wilderness.

By opposing the solutions that have the greatest chance to work, the environmentalists reveal themselves to be unwitting enemies of the planet. We cannot rely on these people to save the earth. Rather, conservatives must assume the responsibility of being the true stewards of creation.

23
Against Gay Marriage

Dear Chris,

Recently I saw a group of gay men marching in a pro-choice rally. They were dressed in the stereotypical style of gay camp, and they carried banners that listed various homosexual organizations and said things like QUEERS FOR CHOICE. I asked myself, what possible interest could homosexuals have in this issue? Then I realized that gay activists hope to legitimize their lifestyle by promoting a view of sexuality that is completely severed from reproduction.

As the political activism of gays today suggests, homosexuality has become an *ideology*. That seems to distinguish it from homosexuality in the past. Among the Greeks, for instance, there were lots of homosexuals. Socrates, I suppose, was a homosexual. But this fact tells us nothing about what Socrates thought about democracy, or about poverty, or about how Greeks should treat

Persians. Now, by contrast, homosexuality has become a worldview.

"There have always been atheists among us," Edmund Burke wrote. "But now they have become turbulent and seditious." This is the way I feel about the gay movement. Following in the path of the civil rights movement, the gay activists have developed a shrewd three-step maneuver. The first step is Tolerance. Here the argument is, "You may think we are strange and disgusting, but put up with us." And many Americans go along with this. Then the gay activists move to stage two. This step may be called Neutrality, and it involves a stronger claim: "You should make no distinction between heterosexuality and homosexuality." If heterosexuals can marry and adopt children, for example, gays should also be able to do so. If this step is conceded, the gays are ready to advance to stage three. This step may be termed Subsidy. "We have been discriminated against for centuries, so now we want preferential treatment." The military, for instance, could be required to admit a certain percentage of gays every year in much the same way that it enforces goals and quotas for women.

The big issue now is, of course, the issue of gay marriage. It does not appear that very many gays want to marry. The reason for this seems fairly obvious: Marriage could put a serious crimp in the promiscuous lifestyle of many male homosexuals. But gay activists have lined up behind the marriage cause, partly to collect health benefits and other legal advantages conferred by marriage, but mostly to gain full social recognition for homosexuality. The real goal of the gay movement is to break down moral resistance to the homosexual lifestyle. Already gays have made considerable progress in this area. Not long ago homosexuality was considered an illness. Now moral criticism of homosexuality is described by gay partisans as a kind of psychological disorder. The person who has moral qualms about homosexual behavior is said to be "homophobic."

Should gays be allowed to marry? Perhaps the most ingenious argument in favor of this has been offered by journalist Andrew Sullivan. Sullivan concedes that some elements of the gay male lifestyle, such as reckless promiscuity, endanger society as well as the lives of the homosexuals who live this way. Sullivan argues, however, that it is social ostracism that marginalizes homosexuals, especially male homosexuals, and makes them behave in this manner. If gays are allowed to be part of society—engaging in its normal rituals, like marriage—then Sullivan is confident that this outrageous element of gay culture would diminish. Sullivan's argument can be condensed to the slogan "Marriage civilizes men."

But Sullivan is wrong. *Marriage* doesn't civilize men, *women* do. Ronald Reagan made this point many years ago. If not for women, he said, men would still be running around in animal skins and wielding clubs. Reagan's point was that male nature needs to be tamed, and that the taming is done by women. I agree completely with Reagan on this point. Untamed male nature can be witnessed in the lifestyle of gay men who have had hundreds, if not thousands, of anonymous sex partners. Female nature is something quite different, and once again we see it in the gay community. Lesbians seem far more capable than gay men of sustaining long-term relationships.

"But why should we prevent people who love each other from getting married?" This is the argument I hear repeatedly, both from gays and from non-gays. Here is the problem. Marriage is defined as the legal union of two adults of the opposite sex who are unrelated to each other. This is the basic definition. Now let's assume we revise the definition to permit gay marriage. What if a group of Mormons, joined by a group of Muslims, presses for the legalization of polygamy? The argument proceeds along the same lines: "I want to have four wives, because we all love each other." And another man says, "Why shouldn't I be able to marry my sister?" And yet others make more exotic claims: "I love my dog and my dog loves me."

The point is that love is a desirable but not sufficient condition for marriage. Why, then, does society have these specific criteria? Why privilege this particular arrangement and grant it special legal status, including the social recognition and tax benefits that go with it? The reason is that marriage is the incubator of children. It is the only known arrangement for the healthy cultivation of the next generation. Bearing children is one area in which gay couples are inherently deficient. In one incident at Dartmouth, Professor Hart was approached by a homosexual English professor who said to him with intense conviction, "Jeff, I really want to have a son." Hart replied, "Don, I think you're going about it the wrong way."

Andrew Sullivan is not satisfied. He points out that some heterosexual couples can't have children, yet society doesn't prevent them from getting married. This is a bad argument that misunderstands the nature of social rules. Consider this: You have to be sixteen years old to drive and eighteen years old to vote. The reason for the rule is that driving and voting require a certain level of maturity. True, some adults don't have such maturity, yet we don't exclude them. True, some minors could probably drive and vote effectively, but we don't let them. The point is that rules are general propositions based on a presumed connection between the established criteria and the behavior that is desired, even though the result may not always be favorable. And so it is with marriage.

What about adoption? Should gays be allowed to adopt? Yes, under certain circumstances. Certainly I can see why an adoption agency might decide that it is better to place a child with Rosie O'Donnell, the lesbian television host, than to have that child grow up in foster homes. On the other hand, heterosexual two-parent families should in general be preferred to homosexual couples. The reason is that children benefit from having a father and a mother. Children relate differently to dads than to moms. I learned a lot about being a man from my dad. There is no way I could have learned those things if I had been raised by two moms.

Gays in the military? Yes! What could possibly be the problem with this? Do you mean to say that, simply because large numbers of homosexual males are placed in the same barracks where they eat together, shower together, work out together, and sleep together, there's sure to be sexual involvement? Nonsense! I think we can fully expect homosexual behavior to be just as rare in our military facilities as it was in the Spartan wrestling pit. Chris, just because gays are allowed in the military doesn't mean they'll use it as an outlet for their sexual urges. Next homophobes will say that gays shouldn't be ordained as priests because they will take advantage of the altar boys.

24
■ Family Values Since Oedipus

Dear Chris,

I see you found my letter on homosexuals quite amusing. As a libertarian, you say that you have no moral objection to homosexual behavior, only an uncomfortable feeling about it. Even so, Chris, you don't have to support "homosexual rights," because homosexuals as individuals *do* have the same rights as everyone else. Yes, you will say, but what about the right to marry? Homosexuals *do* have the right to marry. They have the right to marry adult members of the opposite sex. Now, they may not avail themselves of that right, in the same way that people who have the right to vote may choose not to vote. But one's refusal to exercise a right does not imply that one does not possess the right. Having said all this, I completely agree with you that the problem of family breakdown in our society has not been caused by homosexuals—it is entirely the fault of heterosexuals.

I am very sorry that we have reached the point where the family has become a political issue because now we have to be "pro-family," and thus we are prevented from telling the whole truth about the family. You see, the family has been a major theme of Western literature, from Sophocles to Shakespeare to Jane Austen to Leo Tolstoy. And one of the major conclusions of this literature is that the family is a *pain*. The family is the locus of pettiness, drabness, and ongoing disagreement. Think of it: You are forced to spend your whole life with a bunch of people you didn't even choose!

Such an arrangement is bound to cause problems. Unfortunately, we cannot publicly discuss those problems because we are "pro-family," and we don't want to give ammunition to those who would undermine the family. The great writers of the West had a more subtle view: They understood that, whatever the tensions inherent in family life, there is no serious alternative to the family. They knew the family is a flawed, but indispensable, institution.

The family is indispensable because children come into the world as barbarians. Over the years, I have come to realize that babies and toddlers are not just ignorant, they are also wicked. This point was also made by Saint Augustine. The church father urges us not to be fooled by infants. They *look* angelic, he writes, but consider how shrill, irascible, and demanding they become when their slightest want goes unfulfilled; notice the malevolence with which they strike out at the nurse. Augustine concludes that babies do not lack the will to do harm, only the strength. So who will civilize these barbarians? Who will teach them knowledge and goodness? There is only one answer: the family.

The West is now facing what has been termed the "crisis of the family." And it is a crisis. Nearly one-third of whites, and more than two-thirds of blacks, are born out of wedlock. Maybe I am using an old-fashioned vocabulary, but bastardy has become a normal feature of American life. Some people object: "Don't say that word. It's a mean word." Yes, but it describes a mean condition. Common sense tells us, and studies have confirmed, that it is not a good thing for children to be raised by a single parent. Such children are more likely to be poor, undisciplined, unsuccessful at school, and psychologically disadvantaged, compared with children from two-parent families.

You ask, what has caused the crisis of the family? And are things getting better or worse?

I can think of three major factors responsible for the decline of traditional families. The first is technological capitalism. The problem began during the Industrial Revolution because it separated the workplace and the home. Before that, most people worked at home. Read Peter Laslett's wonderful book *The World We Have Lost*, a study of pre-industrial England. Laslett shows us how the baker, his wife, his children, his servants, even the journeymen he employed, all worked, ate, and slept under the same roof. In a sense, they were all one family.

But this arrangement was destroyed by the coming of industry. The Industrial Revolution drove the man, and later the woman, out of the house and into the workplace. Naturally, the family was transformed. The first stage of this transformation occurred when the man went to work and his wife stayed home. We consider this the "traditional family," but it is not. It is a transitional stage away from the traditional family and toward what we have now. In our current situation, most American children are born into families in which both parents work outside the home. I cannot help but suspect that this is a dysfunctional system despite the Herculean efforts of many parents to raise their children well within this framework.

Capitalism has also caused problems for the family by producing affluence. I recently finished reading Tom Brokaw's book *The Greatest Generation*, which celebrates the virtues of the generation that grew up in the 1930s and came of age in the 1950s. Certainly the 1950s were a happy decade, one in which America somehow managed to combine prosperity and moral decency. Families remained intact, communities were cohesive, people borrowed sugar from their neighbors. Many conservatives regard the 1950s as a near-perfect past. They would like nothing better than to "go back to the fifties."

Such thinking seems to be short-sighted. Think about this: What made the so-called greatest generation so great? The answer is twofold: the Great Depression, and World War II. The virtues of the greatest generation were the product of scarcity and war; need and hardship produced the admirable courage, sacrifice, and solidarity of the greatest generation. But why did the greatest generation fail? For the greatest generation did fail in one crucial respect: It failed to replicate itself. It could not produce another great generation.

Why not? The obvious answer is affluence. Earlier, I spoke of mass affluence as a social achievement, and it is, but it also has a moral downside. The parents from the greatest generation wanted their children to have the advantages they never had. And in giving their children everything the children wanted, the frugal, self-disciplined, sacrificial generation of World War II produced the spoiled children of the 1960s, the Clinton generation. Not surprisingly, the people in this younger generation did not value the same things as their parents. They were raised under different conditions.

In a capitalist society, people don't stay in one place, they go where the jobs are. This mobility, which is an essential feature of capitalism, necessarily disperses the family. When I was growing up in India, dozens of relatives lived within a two-mile radius of my house. Such a situation is so rare in the United States that it if it occurred at all it would be considered peculiar or unnatural. In many countries, however, the American system—which involves sending one's children away to college with the likely consequence that they will never return home to live and may well end up in another part of the country—would be considered a little weird.

May I mention another great destroyer of family values? I refer, of course, to the automobile. In the days before the car, most Americans lived on farms or in small towns. What protected their virtue may be termed the moral supervision of the community. A man looks out of his window. "Hey, isn't that Jack Farmer's son? What the heck is he doing? Hey, Billy-Bob. Stop that! Get out of there!" This moral ecosystem was destroyed by the automobile. Now, for the first time, people (and especially young people) could escape the moral supervision of their community by fleeing to the anonymity of the city.

I have focused on technological capitalism and how it has undermined family values. Another, more recent, cause of the decline of the family is the welfare state. This point was strikingly put by an African American acquaintance of mine. He said, "The welfare state did to the family what even slavery could not do." At first, I thought he was joking. There is an extensive literature on how bad slavery was for the black family. Under slavery, masters could break up families, sell off children, and so on. No slave state permitted slaves to marry legally. All this is depressingly true.

Yet even so, as the work of Herbert Gutman and others shows, African Americans during slavery struggled against incredible pressures to keep their families together. After emancipation, they went to great lengths to reassemble and unify their families. And the illegitimacy rate for blacks for the next hundred years, from 1865 to

1965, never exceeded 25 percent. This is a tribute to the pro-family values of American blacks.

Since 1965, however, the black illegitimacy rate has soared from 25 percent to nearly 70 percent. Whatever caused this change, it was not slavery. In fact, scholars continue to debate how such deterioration could occur so rapidly. The collapse of the black family came with the passage of civil rights laws, with an expanding welfare state, with affirmative action. The liberals were puzzled. Then Charles Murray published *Losing Ground* in the early 1980s. Murray explained that it was not anomalous to see family breakdown in the era of the welfare state since welfare-state policies were responsible for causing this breakdown.

How? One of the fundamental principles of economics is that when you subsidize something, you get more of it. For more than a generation, American welfare policies subsidized illegitimacy and thus America got more of it. Of course, welfare policies were not intended to promote out-of-wedlock births. They were initially aimed at providing benefits for "widows and orphans." But under the non-judgmental logic of modern liberalism, the criteria were expanded and changed so that every illegitimate child resulted in a cash payment by the government to the mother of that child. The more illegitimate children a woman had, the more money the government awarded her.

A more perverse policy could scarcely be imagined, as Murray showed, but the liberals continued to resist welfare reform.

Conservatives and libertarians have focused on welfare as a prime culprit in family deterioration, but we should recognize that illegitimacy rates have risen throughout the society, and not just for women receiving welfare payments. What this tells us is that family breakdown is not simply a problem of government failure. It is also the product of the vast social and moral changes that have occurred across the spectrum of society. Earlier, I outlined some of those economic and technological changes; now I want to focus on moral change.

America and the West have witnessed a moral revolution since the 1960s. This is a revolution in the name of self-fulfillment, of authenticity, of being true to oneself, of following one's inner voice. Rousseau is the great prophet of this revolution. Before the 1960s, most Americans believed in a moral order in the universe that is external to us and that makes claims on us. This moral consensus began to erode in the 1960s. Today people are much more reluctant to believe in an external moral order; rather, they subscribe to the morality of the inner self. I may not be able to figure out what is right and wrong, but I can dig deep within myself and discover what is right and wrong *for me*.

A half-century ago, when people divorced, they frequently regarded themselves as having failed in one of their most important undertakings in life, and many people in unhappy marriages nevertheless stayed together "for the sake of the children." One may say that whether people got divorced or not, the moral pressure was inevitably on the side of staying, of working it out somehow. What has changed is not that people get divorced but that the moral pressure today is on the side of leaving. Many people feel they cannot possibly stay in a marriage so sterile, they worry that their lives would be a waste if they did, they become convinced that the decision to leave is a mark of courage and independence and perhaps even of liberation. As for the children, they are rarely considered a sufficient reason to keep the marriage together. People contemplating divorce defiantly say, "How could my children be happy when I am unhappy?"

The reason I tell you these things, Chris, is to caution you against the supposition that these economic, social, and moral changes can be easily reversed. Nor would we want to reverse them all. Irving Kristol once quipped that "America does not have a single moral problem that another Great Depression would not cure." This is probably true, but who wants to endure an economic depression in order to improve the moral state of the country? Rather, the preferred objective, it seems to me, is to restore old values under new conditions. In the old days, people borrowed sugar from their neighbors because they didn't have any sugar at home. In previous generations, couples sometimes stayed together because they could not afford to live separately. How do we foster those virtues of intact families and close-knit communities when the circumstances that gave rise to those virtues have changed? This is our dilemma.

One encouraging development is that people continue to want closer families and the sense of community
that made life so meaningful for earlier generations.
Also, technology and affluence are giving more people
the time and the means to foster these relationships. For
instance, you'll notice that in many of America's more
affluent neighborhoods, women don't work outside the
home. The reason is that the additional income would
not significantly change the family lifestyle. These
women—and they are educated women—would prefer
to be stay-at-home moms than career moms. They have
realized the truth of G. K. Chesterton's dictum, "Why
be something to everybody when you can be everything
to somebody?"

Since affluence gives increasing numbers of women
the means to stay at home without losing their standard
of living, it is helping to make the family structure of the
1950s viable again. Also, technology has made it possible
for many women to work part-time at home and for
many men (including me) to work full-time at home.
Thus the separation of home and workplace, caused by
the Industrial Revolution, could be undone over time by
new technologies. Family life is sure to benefit if this
happens.

Finally, a word about government policy. For the
past several decades, foolish government policies have
harmed the family. One example of this is the so-called
"marriage penalty," in which couples filing a joint return
pay a higher tax rate on their combined income than

they would pay if they had filed individually. Another example is government programs that have encouraged illegitimacy by paying women to have children out of wedlock.

These policies have come under severe attack, and even many liberals have come to understand that they are destructive. And so we have had welfare reform, and there are several proposals to make our tax law more marriage-friendly. These changes are all to the good, and it makes perfect sense for government policy to seek to strengthen the family—an institution that is the primary incubator of morals and the "school of civilization" for the young. Let us not, however, expect these reforms, even when they are all enacted, to fully restore "the world we have lost." That world, I am afraid, is gone forever, and the best we can do is to preserve aspects of it in the new world that we inhabit now.

25
■ Speaking As a Former Fetus . . .

Dear Chris,

I knew the time would come when you would ask me about the abortion issue. This is a hard one, and I am by no means an expert on the subject. I have learned a great deal about it, strangely enough, by studying the Lincoln-Douglas debates. These debates were about slavery. But look how closely the arguments parallel the abortion debate.

Douglas, the Democrat, took the pro-choice position. He said that each state should decide for itself whether it wanted slavery. Douglas denied that he was pro-slavery. In fact, at one time he professed to be "personally opposed" to it. All the same, Douglas was reluctant to impose his moral views on the new territories; instead, he affirmed the right of each state to choose. He invoked the great principle of freedom of choice.

Lincoln, the Republican, disagreed. Lincoln argued that choice cannot be exercised without reference to the content of the choice. How can it make sense to permit a person to choose to enslave another human being? How can self-determination be invoked to deny others self-determination? How can choice be used to negate choice? At its deepest level, Lincoln was saying that the legitimacy of freedom as a political principle is itself dependent on a doctrine of natural rights that arises out of a specific understanding of human nature and human dignity.

If Negroes are like hogs, Lincoln said, then the pro-choice position is right, and there is no problem with choosing to own them. Of course they may be governed without their consent. But if Negroes are human beings, then it is grotesquely evil to treat them like hogs, to buy and sell them as objects of merchandise.

The argument between Douglas and Lincoln is similar in content, and very nearly in form, to the argument between the pro-choice and the pro-life movements. Pro-choice advocates don't like to be considered pro-abortion. Many of them say they are "personally opposed." One question to put to them is, "*Why* are you personally opposed?" The only reason for one to be personally opposed to abortion is that one is deeply convinced that the fetus is more than a mere collection of cells, that it is a developing human being.

Even though the weight of the argument is strongly on the pro-life side, the pro-choice side seems to be winning politically. This is because liberals understand that abortion-on-demand is the debris of the sexual revolution. If you are going to have sexual promiscuity, then there are going to be mistakes, and many women are going to get pregnant without wanting to do so. For them, the fetus becomes what one feminist writer termed "an uninvited guest." As long as the fetus occupies the woman's womb, liberals view it as an enemy of female autonomy. Thus liberalism is willing to grant the woman full control over the life of the fetus, even to the point of allowing her to kill it. No other liberal principle, not equality, not compassion, is permitted to get in the way of the principle of autonomy.

The abortion issue reveals the bloody essence of modern liberalism. In fact, it is the one issue on which liberals rarely compromise. Being pro-choice is a litmus test for nomination to high office in the Democratic Party. Liberals as a group oppose *any* restriction of abortion. They don't want laws that regulate late-term abortion. Many liberals object to parental notification laws because they require that parents be alerted if a minor seeks to have an abortion. Some liberals would even allow partial-birth abortion, a gruesome procedure in which the abortionist dismembers a child who could survive outside the womb. One may say that in the church of modern liberalism, abortion has become a sacrament.

What, then, is the challenge facing the pro-life movement? It is the same challenge that Lincoln faced: to build popular consent for the restriction and ultimately the ending of abortions. Right now the pro-life movement does not enjoy the support it needs from the American people to do this. Neither, by the way, did Lincoln have a national mandate to end slavery. It is highly significant that Lincoln was not an abolitionist. He was resolutely antislavery in principle, but his political campaign focused on the issue of curtailing the spread of slavery to the territories.

In my view, the pro-life movement at this point should focus on seeking to reduce the number of abortions. At times this will require political and legal fights; at times it will require education and the establishment of alternatives to abortion, such as adoption centers. Unfortunately, such measures are sometimes opposed by so-called hard-liners in the pro-life movement. These hard-liners are fools. Because they want to outlaw *all* abortions, they refuse to settle for stopping *some* abortions; the consequence is that they end up preventing *no* abortions. These folks should learn some lessons from Abraham Lincoln.

26
■ The Hypocrisy of Anti-Globalists

Dear Chris,

I see from your letter that the anti-globalist cause is gaining momentum at your university. You comment on the number of "beautiful airheads" who are showing up at campus rallies and mouthing anti-globalist slogans. Well, we know the cause has become fashionable when the pretty girls show up.

Fashionable, however, is not the same thing as reasonable. To hear the anti-globalists tell it, disruptions of trade meetings and international conferences are justified because the protesters are speaking out for poor workers in the Third World. In their view, poor people in Thailand, India, Nigeria, and other Third World countries are being exploited by free trade and global capitalism. How cruel, they say, that a multinational company that would have to pay an American worker $16 an hour can get away with paying a Third World worker a meager $5 a day. Moral indignation suffuses the breast of the anti-globalist.

But this moral indignation is a bit of a pose. Indeed, it is a rhetorical camouflage for the basest hypocrisy on the part of the protesters. To see why this is so, let us begin with the charge that companies are exploiting foreign workers by paying them appallingly low wages. Five dollars a day seems like an outrage by American standards, but is it unjust for Coca-Cola, Levi Strauss, or General Electric to pay that much to workers in a country where the going rate is $3 a day, and where things cost much less than they do in America?

Anyone who has lived in a Third World country, as I have, knows that when multinational corporations advertise for jobs, there are long lines of applicants. The reason is simple: As Edward Graham of the Institute for International Economics documents, multinational companies offer the best-paying jobs around. Some anti-globalists are skeptical about this, but why would Third World workers work for multinationals unless they were being offered a better deal than they could get elsewhere?

Not only do free trade policies help foreign workers at Coca Cola and General Electric, they also help other families in Third World countries because the increased demand for labor pushes up wages even for workers who are not employed by multinational corporations. Thus countries that have embraced globalization, such as China and India, have seen growth rates of 5 percent or more per year, compared with 2 percent in Western countries, and 1 percent or less in countries outside the free-trade loop. Free trade and globalization have helped millions of Third World people enjoy the amenities of a middle-class lifestyle.

But perhaps the anti-globalists think that the multinationals could do better. Why not mandate higher wages for Third World workers? Come to think of it, why not require that they be paid the same rate as American workers? The obvious reason is that under such laws Coca-Cola, Nike, and General Electric would prefer not to use Third World labor at all. Multinationals hire Third World workers because they are much cheaper to employ than their First World counterparts.

Admittedly, a Thai worker making shoes for $5 a day is likely to pose a competitive threat to an American worker doing the same job for $12 an hour. Alarmed by this prospect, American unions are fighting desperately to protect their members from foreign competition. One textile union even opposes measures to open American markets to Asian and African textiles. In supporting restrictive tariffs and trade barriers, the unions realize that they are in direct opposition to the aspirations of Third World peoples seeking to raise their living standard through trade with the West.

In this fight, American unions have found an unlikely ally: columnist and sometime presidential candidate Patrick Buchanan. To permit foreign workers to compete with Americans, Buchanan writes in *The Death of the West*, "is to betray our own workers and their families. We should put America first." Buchanan's argument is basically tribal: We should uphold the interests of our steel, shoe, and textile workers at the expense of the rest of the world, whose economic welfare is not our concern.

Much as I disagree with Buchanan, let's at least credit the man for being honest. He doesn't give a damn about the Third World, and he is willing to say so. Such candor is woefully absent from the vast majority of anti-globalists, who pretend to be fighting on behalf of the Third World while in fact they are undermining the interests of Third World people. This is the hypocrisy that many of us with Third World backgrounds find really sickening. No wonder that ordinary people from Asia, Africa, and Latin America are conspicuously absent from demonstrations against globalization. Poor people from the Third World increasingly ask: With the anti-globalists for friends, who needs enemies?

27
■ Are Immigrants to Blame?

Dear Chris,

Good news: Your suggestion that I turn these letters into a book is bearing fruit. I have been meeting with Liz Maguire, my former editor at the Free Press, who is now at Basic Books, and she is interested. So, Chris, you may be seeing your name in print quite soon, and our candid exchanges may be presented to a much wider audience. I hope you realize that this completely ends any hopes you might have for running for public office.

In your last letter you asked me to say something about the issue of immigrants. It's obviously an issue that I've thought about a lot. I think about it every time I hear a multicultural half-wit repeat the mantra that "all cultures are equal." Every immigrant knows that this is a lie. For what is the immigrant doing but voting with his feet—in the most dramatic way possible—against his culture and in favor of a new culture? The immigrant would never leave his family, his friends, and his country unless he was firmly convinced that, on balance, the new culture was fundamentally *better* than the old culture. The immigrant is a walking refutation of cultural relativism.

Why do immigrants come to America? One reason is to have more opportunity, to have a better life. Only in America could Pierre Omidyar, whose parents are from Iran and who grew up in France, have started eBay and become a business legend. Only in America could Vinod Khosla, the son of an Indian army officer, have become the shaper of the global technology industry and a billionaire to boot. Every country looks after its rich guys. America, more than any other country, gives the ordinary guy a good life and a chance at success.

But material success is only half the reason why immigrants come to America. For many immigrants, the biggest change that America produces in their lives is not material. Sure, they live better here, but it is not a fundamental difference. The larger difference is that in their home countries their destiny would, to a large degree, have been given to them. In America, they craft it for themselves. What to become, whom to love, whom to marry, which church to go to, which beliefs to espouse—these are things that, in America, we decide for ourselves. Here we are the architects of our own destiny.

So America is good for immigrants. But are the immigrants good for America? Should America allow in nearly 1 million legal immigrants every year? First let me say that every country has a right to determine whether it wants to take immigrants, how many it wants to take, and what kind of immigrants it seeks. There is no automatic "right" to admission as an immigrant. The immigrant may want to come, but the country in question must want to take him.

Many Americans are ambivalent. Indeed, a majority of Americans seems convinced that current immigration levels should be reduced. The opposition to immigration comes from within both political parties; it comes both from the left and from the right. From the left, the opposition is mainly on economic grounds. From the right, it is mainly on cultural grounds.

The critics of immigration are wrong. Immigrants provide economic benefits to America by taking jobs that most Americans refuse to take. Immigrants clean people's homes, serve as nannies, do agricultural labor, flip hamburgers, and drive taxis in New York and Washington, D.C. These services are affordable to many Americans only because immigrant labor is relatively cheap. In addition to doing these low-level jobs, immigrants also provide specialized labor that America needs. Immigrant doctors, engineers, and high-tech entrepreneurs and programmers have contributed immeasurably to America's economic and social well-being.

True, immigrant workers who are willing to work for $6 an hour tend to out-compete native-born American workers who want to be paid $10 an hour for doing the same work. Why, then, is the immigrant willing to work for less? Because he is typically comparing America to his home country. If wages in Sri Lanka are only $6 a day, the Sri Lankan immigrant is delighted to work for $6 an hour. As a result, the products and services provided with the help of immigrant labor are considerably cheaper than they would be had they been produced by native-born labor. In economic terms, immigration hurts some American workers, but it also benefits a larger group of American consumers.

I believe the stronger argument against immigration is cultural. I recently debated Pat Buchanan on this question on David Gergen's PBS television show. Buchanan bewailed the moral and cultural decline of the West, as suggested by such indices as divorce, illegitimacy, crime rates, pornography, homosexuality, and so on. Then he proceeded to blame immigrants for America's problems. But as I tried to point out to Buchanan, his statement was a non sequitur. Who caused America's cultural decline? Not the immigrants! America's cultural decline was caused by its natives.

Buchanan had to admit this was true. He had a harder time admitting that immigrants are frequently the *solution* to this cultural and moral decline. Immigrants often have very strong family values, as shown by low divorce and illegitimacy rates. Immigrants have a strong work ethic and practice the virtues of frugality and deferred gratification. Immigrants are naturally patriotic because they know how much better their lives are in America than they would be in their home countries.

I am not suggesting that all immigrants are like this. By and large, if I may say so, the farther that people travel to get to America, the better the quality of the immigrant. Immigrants from Thailand are, in general, greater assets to America than immigrants from Tijuana. This is not because the Thai are better people than the Mexicans. Rather, the reason is that it takes greater courage, entrepreneurship, and ingenuity to get to America from Thailand than from Tijuana.

I mention this because I would like to see America's immigration policy become more selective. Canada and Australia are not too bashful to say, "We want doctors. We want nannies. We want investors. So those are the kind of people we are going to take." America's immigration policy has a different emphasis: family unification. But this provision, though well intentioned, is open to endless abuse. Over his lifetime, an immigrant can bring tens or even hundreds of relatives to America under the guise of "family unification." This is how it works: I bring my parents. Then I sponsor my brother and sister. My siblings then bring their spouses. The spouses then bring their parents. And so on. The chain of family unification extends indefinitely.

Greater selectivity is also needed for American immigration policy today because there is a new magnet for immigrants that didn't exist in the past: the welfare state. A century ago, immigrants came to America for opportunity; now, some come for a free ride. And this is fundamentally unjust to native-born Americans. Whatever the merits of the welfare state, it is intended to settle accounts between Americans. Certainly Americans don't owe welfare-state entitlements to people who come here from other countries.

Some liberal Democratic politicians, however, dangle the welfare state as a bribe in an attempt to buy immigrant votes. Several years ago, I attended a reception sponsored by some Indian American group at which Charles Schumer—then a congressman, now the senior senator from New York—spoke. Schumer told the Indian Americans that they had been in the country for many years, but they were still acting like guests. By this he meant that the Indians worked hard and behaved themselves, but they did not make demands of the American political system. They did not raise hell, and they did not seek government benefits and favors. Schumer's point was that we should do these things! And he was there to provide those services! In this way do power-seeking politicians seek to corrupt immigrants.

Another effective technique for ruining immigrants is multiculturalism. In previous generations, immigrants who came to America were expected to assimilate. The results were spectacular: Immigrants changed America and were changed by America. Some people called it the melting pot. It worked.

Today the liberals and the multiculturalists tell immigrants that they should not try to "become American." They should continue to speak their native languages, they should demand bilingual programs so their children can study in Spanish, Chinese, or Tagalog. They should affirm their ethnic identities and refuse to be integrated into a common culture.

This is destructive for America and bad for immigrants. What prospects does a Tagalog speaker have in the American work force? Most immigrants, of course, recognize this. They come here because they want the American way of life. If they had wanted the Pakistani way of life, they would have remained in Pakistan. But of course they feel pangs of loneliness, isolation, nostalgia, and so on. The liberals and the multiculturalists exploit that. Instead of helping immigrants to make the necessary but difficult transition from one way of life to another, they seek to seduce immigrants into remaining separate and holding fast to their old identities. Buchanan and others are right to be outraged about this. But the answer is to keep multiculturalism away from immigrants, not to keep immigrants away from America.

America can and should have a generous immigration policy. But it should be a more selective policy in which America specifies the kind of professions and the kind of people it wants and needs. Moreover, America's immigration policy should be part of a reconstructed cultural framework in which immigrants are encouraged, indeed expected, to embrace the ideals of America and to adapt to the American way of life.

28
■ Why Liberals Hate America

Dear Chris,

I am not surprised that your political science professor thinks George Bush is leading America into a "quagmire." I am sure he learned that big word during the Vietnam era. No doubt the earnest fellow is also telling your class that America should not "rush to military solutions" but instead "give peace a chance." Ordinarily this Kumbayah mentality amuses me for its naïve idiocy. But behind it there is an anti-American prejudice that I find less risible. This anti-American strain also goes back to Vietnam; although less conspicuous today, it remains an influential element of leftist thought.

It is not, of course, anti-American to question American actions. I do not subscribe to the mindless patriotism that asserts, "My country, right or wrong." Liberalism crosses the line from criticism to anti-Americanism when it shows a pathological hatred of

America, and when it faults the United States for offenses that it routinely excuses in the nation's enemies. Recently I debated the novelist Gore Vidal on PBS. Summoning up all his venom, Vidal denounced the United States as a "rogue nation" and even suggested that Osama bin Laden's terrorist attack was a preemptive strike to thwart a pending American invasion of Afghanistan. (This American plot seems to have resided entirely in Vidal's imagination.)

Vidal's pique may be attributable to personal causes, but the "blame America first" mentality it conveys is prevalent on the left. Consider the common liberal assertion that America purports to stand for such noble ideals as human rights while in reality America nakedly pursues its own self-interest. Liberals are quick to sneer that the Gulf War was fought not to promote the freedom of Kuwaitis but to protect American access to Middle Eastern oil. Liberal intellectuals take pleasure in showing how America has historically invoked democratic ideals while supporting dictators such as Anastasio Somoza in Nicaragua, Augusto Pinochet in Chile, Ferdinand Marcos in the Philippines, and the Shah of Iran. Even now, liberals tirelessly point out, America is supporting unelected regimes in Pakistan, Egypt, and Saudi Arabia.

How valid are these claims? As a patriot, Chris, you may be tempted to defend America on all counts and to deny that its policies are rooted in self-interest. Resist this temptation. There is nothing wrong with admit-

ting that America, like other countries, acts on behalf
of its own citizens. Think about this: The people in a
democratic society empower their government to act in
their interest. Why should their elected representatives
be neutral between their interests and, say, the interests
of the Somalians? To ask a nation to ignore its own
self-interest is tantamount to asking it to put aside the
welfare of its people. Liberals seem to think it is outrageous for America to pursue its self-interest even as
they recognize that other countries pursue their self-
interest.

Despite this reality of foreign policy, Americans can
be proud of how often their country's actions have si-
multaneously protected American interests while also
advancing universal ideals and the welfare of other peoples. While the United States was careful to wait until it
was directly attacked before entering into World War II,
American involvement in the war helped accelerate the
defeat of the Axis powers and advanced the freedom and
security of the whole world. So, too, America's involvement in the Gulf War was partly intended to protect
American oil interests, but it was also aimed at expelling
a barbarous invader from Kuwait. In these instances
America's interests did not corrupt American ideals;
rather, the ideals ennobled the interests.

But what about American support for Somoza,
Pinochet, Marcos, and the Shah? This support is fully
justified when we consider the operating principle of
foreign policy. Foreign policy is not a philosophy semi-

nar. In philosophy seminars, the choice is usually between good and evil. In the real world, however, the choice is often between a bad guy and a worse guy. The central principle of foreign policy is the doctrine of the lesser evil. This means that a country is always justified in supporting a bad regime to overthrow a regime that is even worse. In World War II, for instance, the United States allied with a very bad man, Joseph Stalin, to oppose a man who was an even greater threat at the time, Adolf Hitler.

By the same logic, U.S. support for despots such as Pinochet, Marcos, and the Shah of Iran was entirely defensible in the context of the cold war. The United States was fighting a larger battle against the "evil empire." Given that the Soviet empire posed the greatest threat to freedom and human rights in the world, the United States was right to attach less significance to the status of Pinochet, Marcos, and the Shah as tin-pot dictators than to their anti-Soviet beliefs.

But now the cold war is over, so why is America supporting unelected regimes in Pakistan, Egypt, and Saudi Arabia? Once again, the liberal fails to ask the relevant question: What is the alternative? During the 1970s, Jimmy Carter decided that the longtime ally of the United States, the Shah of Iran, was a despot. Applying typical liberal logic, Carter decided that he could not in good conscience continue to support the Shah. Indeed, he actively aided in the Shah's ouster. The result, of course, was the reign of the Ayatollah Khomeini. If the

Shah was bad, Khomeini was worse. To avoid this kind of disaster, America should be slow to destabilize the flawed regimes of Pakistan, Egypt, and Saudi Arabia until it is confident that the alternative is a pro-Western liberal democracy. More likely, the alternative will be Islamic fundamentalism of the bin Laden stripe.

Are liberals incapable of the kind of practical moral reasoning that foreign policy requires? It seems that they are. Most liberals are content with slogans that cannot survive the slightest scrutiny. "Violence never solves problems." This is manifestly not true. Violence helped to end the regimes of Adolf Hitler and Benito Mussolini. The atomic bombs dropped on Hiroshima and Nagasaki, however controversial their use, did solve the big problem of an unyielding Japan. Violence proved equally effective against the Taliban. "But you can't impose democracy at the point of a bayonet." This is another liberal shibboleth. In reality, at the end of World War II, America imposed democracy at the point of a bayonet on Japan and Germany, and it has proved a resounding success in both countries. The problem with liberals is that they never give bayonets a chance.

29
■ A Republican Realignment?

Dear Chris,

America has a one-party system of government. I mean this in a special sense: One party tends to dominate American politics in a given era. One major party sets the agenda, and the other party has the choice of reactively opposing its ideas, or of sounding a feeble cry of "me, too." During the Andrew Jackson era, the Democrats were the majority party. This dominance lasted half a century, until the Civil War. After the war, the Republicans became the majority camp, a position they held until the Great Depression. Since 1932, the Democrats assumed the majority position, which was consolidated during the Roosevelt years, and continued even through the Reagan years. Only in 1994, when the Republicans won both houses of Congress, did the Democrats lose the majority status they had enjoyed for most of the twentieth century. The big question now is, Can the Republicans secure a new majority that will carry them through the first half of the twenty-first century?

It was Ronald Reagan who showed the Republican Party the way to its current success. Before Reagan, the GOP was the party of balanced budgets. Republicans used to fault the Democrats' programs as well-meaning but fiscally irresponsible. Consequently, Republicans sought to limit the programs so that spending could be kept in line with revenues. Another way that Republicans sought fiscal stability was by proposing tax increases. Thus the Republican Party earned a well-deserved reputation for being the party that a) raised your taxes, and b) reduced your government benefits. The Republicans were Scrooge, and the Democrats were Santa Claus. Not surprisingly, Republicans lost election after election.

Reagan changed this dynamic. His belief was that if the Democrats wanted to spend money, the Republicans would refuse to accommodate them by raising taxes. Let the Democrats be the party of tax increases. The Republicans would be for tax cuts. The Reagan tax cuts had an economic rationale: to give people the incentive to produce more. But lower tax rates also had the political effect of limiting the revenues available to the Democrats for spending. Essentially, Reagan took away their allowance. He gave the Democrats the choice of enduring huge and growing deficits with interest payments that would eat into future spending, or of going on a fiscal diet to limit the size of the deficits. The Democrats chose the second course, which explains one of the most remarkable political reversals of recent decades. Suddenly the Democrats became the party of tax increases and balanced budgets.

Since Reagan, the Republican Party has suffered what may be termed the problem of success. Reagan was too successful: His efforts helped to end the cold war and to secure the triumph of capitalism over socialism. Consequently, Reagan took these issues off the table. When Reagan's appointed successor, George Bush, showed that during his eight years as vice president he had learned virtually nothing from Reagan, the American people hurled him out of office and ushered in the Clinton people; they proceeded to rent out the Lincoln bedroom, sell presidential pardons, seduce the interns, and do all the low, deviant things that the Clinton people are known to do.

Despite his disgraceful personal conduct, Bill Clinton was not a bad president. He fought for a landmark free trade agreement, signed welfare reform, and moved the Democratic Party to the political center. Republicans loathed him, and against their political interests they tried to impeach him. Consider this: Had the GOP succeeded in kicking Clinton out of office, Al Gore would have become president, he would have proclaimed himself a healer, and he would have been invincible in the election of 2000. Republican leaders kept wailing that Clinton was "stealing" their issues. They didn't know what Reagan knew: that one of the greatest achievements in politics is to make your opponent do what you would do if you were in power. So the Republicans flailed ineffectively against Clinton, but his high approval ratings prevented them from ousting the rogue.

Even so, by the year 2000, Americans were frustrated with the low tone that had become endemic to American politics, and they took out their frustration with Clinton—on Al Gore. Although George W. Bush entered the White House under the most harrowing of circumstances, he proceeded to campaign for a bold tax cut, which he got. Then came the terrorist attacks of September 11, 2001, and Bush underwent what can only be termed a metamorphosis. Suddenly the mumbling, bumbling Texan emerged as a firm, articulate national leader.

Despite Bush's continuing popularity, the Republican Party faces two big challenges that it must address if it is going to win enduring majority status. The first challenge is that affluent people are no longer voting solidly Republican. It used to be an iron law of politics that, as people became well-off, they became Republicans. (The only exception to this law was Jews, who maintained a tradition of loyalty to liberal causes. Irving Kristol once observed that Jews were the only people who earned like Episcopalians and voted like Puerto Ricans.) But for every other group, the iron law held. Now, however, affluent people are as likely to vote Democrat as Republican. The reason is that, as people become richer, they become more conservative economically but more liberal socially. Wealth gives people more choices, and people who have choices do not like rules that seek to limit what they choose. Consequently, the new affluent class is disposed to vote for Democrats who are economically centrist but who will let them live as they want.

If Republicans are to become a lasting majority, they must win the votes of affluent suburbanites. To do this, they must convince the country that they are not the party of moral naysayers, and they are not merely a front for the Christian Right. I am not suggesting that the Republicans relinquish their moral beliefs. The Republican Party is the party of values, and this can be a great asset if Republicans find the right language in which to speak about values. Throughout the country, there is a widespread belief that the American standard of living has gone up but values have gone down. The Republican Party needs to capitalize on this conviction without sounding extreme or harsh.

The second Republican challenge involves immigrants and minorities. Right now, nine out of ten blacks and two out of three immigrants vote for Democrats. Indeed, it is often counted as an achievement when a Republican candidate wins 30 percent of the Hispanic vote, as George W. Bush did. If these trends continue, they will prove to be an electoral disaster for the GOP. Republicans have been trying to address this problem by making histrionic displays of diversity at GOP events and by adopting various forms of "outreach" to blacks and Hispanics. I have heard it solemnly asserted at GOP events that African Americans are natural Republicans because they are quite conservative.

Yes, African Americans are slightly more conservative than white Americans on social issues such as abortion and school prayer. The problem is that African Americans do not vote on these issues. They vote on one issue: race. Wealthy blacks are just as likely as poor blacks to vote for the Democratic candidate. The reason is simple: The Democrats are willing to give blacks more goodies. Republicans cannot compete in this governmental auction; they are sure to lose. Therefore, in my view, Republicans should recognize that in the short term there is no way to win the black vote. What they should do, therefore, is allow the Democratic Party to be the party of blacks and black demands. Republicans can build a winning multiracial coalition based on economic growth, national unity, merit, and color-blindness.

In this area Republicans should focus on increasing their share of the Hispanic vote and on winning the Asian American vote. Asian Americans have a natural home in the Republican Party. They succeed in America mainly through merit. As immigrants who have chosen to come here, they tend to be very patriotic. No other group is as socially conservative: Divorce and illegitimacy are rare in the Asian American community. Asian American values—frugality, hard work, and deferred gratification—are precisely the values that Republicans champion. Yet mysteriously the Republicans are getting only 30–35 percent of Asian American votes. The GOP should be getting 90 percent. If Republicans can get 40 percent of the Hispanic vote and decisively capture the Asian American vote, they will win virtually every election.

In general, the Republican Party can succeed through a Reaganite combination of philosophical conservatism and temperamental geniality. (Too many Republicans are philosophically insecure and temperamentally forbidding.) The general conservative themes of limited government, strong defense, equal rights under the law, and traditional values continue to be enormously attractive to people. The Republican agenda for the next several years is pretty clear: Defeat terrorism, enact a flat tax, give parents educational choice, eliminate race and gender preferences, and allow Social Security contributions to be invested in private accounts.

If Republicans do these things, and make their case to the American people, they will become the majority party for the next half century.

30
Why Conservatives Should Be Cheerful

Dear Chris,

Among young people there is the perception that conservatives are stuffy and lugubrious, and that liberals are easygoing and fun loving. At one time this may have been true, but it is not true any more. Admittedly, a few on the right are always giving vent to frustration and gloom. But in general, I have found that conservatives tend to be much more cheerful than liberals.

The predominant liberal emotion is indignation. When I was at the *Dartmouth Review* the majority of letters we received from liberals began with the sentence, "I am shocked and appalled." Liberals are always "shocked and appalled" by something. By contrast, the predominant conservative emotion is the horselaugh. The conservative is one who chuckles and guffaws. Some who have observed this levity on the right are puzzled by it. Conservatives, after all, tend to believe in the weakness, if not depravity, of human nature. The cultural pessimists have given us a depressing portrait of moral and cultural decline. Consequently, one would expect the natural temperament of conservatives to be one of cultural and moral despair. So why are conservatives so cheerful and upbeat?

The issue of moral and cultural decline is a real one, and it will provide conservatism with its greatest challenge. Conservatives must not only conserve what is good but also provide arguments for rebuilding institutions—such as the church and the family—that have lost much of their traditional influence and rationale. Even so, there is no reason to panic, because we are fully up to the task. We are justified in being upbeat because we know that we are in the right, and that the right will eventually prevail.

Already conservatives have won stunning victories. Imagine if conservatives had assembled a national conference in 1980, the year Reagan was elected, and set forth the goals that they reasonably intended to accomplish in two decades. They might have resolved to push the Soviet Union out of Afghanistan. They might have hoped to scale back on some government programs. They might have expected to make headway in convincing people that capitalism is better than socialism.

But who could have reasonably expected the collapse of the entire Soviet empire? Who could have foreseen the utter discrediting of socialism? Who could have known that the Republicans would take both houses of Congress? Or that welfare as an entitlement would cease to exist? Or that liberalism would be put completely on the defensive, while conservatives set the national agenda? These are spectacular victories, and they have emboldened many conservatives to believe that they are now on the winning side.

Conservatives have also discovered that a few people can change the agenda, and the country, with a powerful idea. A good example of this is the critique of affirmative action. When I first started writing about this issue a decade ago, racial preferences had become completely institutionalized. The issue seemed settled and the controversy over it destined to subside as people became reconciled to affirmative action.

The critics of race and gender preferences were so few that they could be counted on two hands. By contrast, the other side had legions of troops and enormous institutional resources. Moreover, there was a disproportion of incentives. The foes of affirmative action had no personal stake in the issue. If affirmative action ended, we gained nothing. By contrast, the other side had jobs and promotions and government contracts at stake. They could be expected to fight hard to preserve these privileges.

Even so, the critics of affirmative action have made huge inroads, and the momentum is with us. We have not only succeeded in putting the issue on the national agenda but also forced the opposition onto the defensive, and we have won impressive victories in the courts. Slowly but surely, the courts have narrowed the circumstances in which race and gender preferences may be legally used, and it is now possible to envision the day when they are completely struck down.

There is a reason for conservatives to be cheerful, however, that goes beyond the contingencies of the time. Indeed, I venture to suggest that conservatives would remain upbeat even if none of the victories I have charted had occurred. Moreover, I believe that liberals would persist in being outraged and indignant even if they had not suffered the startling reversals of the past couple of decades.

But how can these things be so, given that liberals have an optimistic view of human nature and conservatives have a pessimistic view of human nature? It is precisely because liberals believe in the goodness and malleability of human nature that they are perennially outraged when this nature proves resistant to liberal reforms. It is precisely because conservatives believe that human nature is flawed that they have modest expectations about people, and about politics. Thus, when things turn out not so badly, conservatives are pleased. People who expect the deluge are always delighted that all they have to endure is an occasional thunderstorm.

So, fight on with a cheerful disposition, Chris. I realize that at times the battles seem never-ending and the odds appear long. There is an old Tibetan saying, "After crossing the mountain . . . more mountains!" Those of us who have journeyed across harsh political terrain know the feeling. But we also know that truth is on our side and that it is a very powerful weapon. With truth as our guide and courage in our hearts, we will not only endure, we will prevail.

31
■ A Conservative Reading List

Dear Chris,

To be an educated conservative, you have to be familiar with the "best that has been thought and said" of modern conservative thought. Here, then, is my list of the most important works produced in the past half century or so that a young conservative should read. My list includes books written by conservatives as well as books that discuss themes that are important to conservatism. Some writers who would not call themselves conservatives, including Margaret Mead and George Orwell, are on the list. I should caution you that this is not a comprehensive catalog; it is necessarily biased toward books that I have found persuasive and profound. Finally, I have kept the list brief, because life is short.

Robert Bork, *The Tempting of America* (1990): The single best critique of liberal jurisprudence, and an argument for interpreting the Constitution by consulting the intentions of the framers.

Allan Bloom, *The Closing of the American Mind* (1987): A great teacher's learned account of how our best young minds came to the conclusion that there are no truths.

Patrick Buchanan, *Right from the Beginning* (1988): A pugnacious and absorbing account of how the author came of age as a conservative.

Whittaker Chambers, *Witness* (1952): A profoundly personal and deeply moving account of one man's liberation from the shackles of Communism.

George Gilder, *Men and Marriage* (1986): An iconoclastic argument for why "women's liberation" produces angry women and emasculated men.

Milton Friedman, *Capitalism and Freedom* (1962): Capitalism's most powerful advocate in recent decades makes his argument for the free market.

Friedrich Hayek, *The Road to Serfdom* (1944): This hugely influential book shows the similarities between Communism and fascism and makes one of the first and best defenses of libertarian individualism.

Paul Hollander, *Political Pilgrims* (1981): A devastating account of the gullibility and outright stupidity of prominent liberal intellectuals who made pilgrimages to Stalin's Russia, Mao's China, and Castro's Cuba.

Harry Jaffa, *The Crisis of the House Divided* (1959): Through an examination of the Lincoln-Douglas debates, this book offers deep and subtle reflections on the exercise of political statesmanship.

Russell Kirk, *The Conservative Mind: From Burke to Eliot* (1953): A broad survey of the intellectual breadth of conservative thought, with a special emphasis on Edmund Burke.

Irving Kristol, *Neoconservatism: The Autobiography of an Idea* (1995): Learned and incisive essays by a former liberal who was "mugged by reality" and moved right.

Peter Laslett, *The World We Have Lost* (1965): This study of England before the Industrial Revolution shows the virtues, and the limitations, of the world that was transformed by technological capitalism.

Ludwig von Mises, *Human Action* (1949): Why capitalism works and socialism doesn't, by the great man of Austrian economics.

Margaret Mead, *Male and Female* (1949): A comprehensive and politically incorrect survey of sex differences and their social consequences.

Charles Murray, *Losing Ground* (1984): One of the best arguments against the welfare state, this book became the intellectual blueprint for welfare reform.

George Nash, *The Conservative Intellectual Movement in America Since 1945* (1976): A useful historical account of how American conservatism went from obscure philosophizing to a mainstream political movement.

Peggy Noonan, *What I Saw at the Revolution* (1991): A wonderfully revealing book that tells the reader a lot about Reagan, and a lot about Peggy.

Michael Oakeshott, *Rationalism in Politics and Other Essays* (1962): The limits of social engineering and of rational blueprints for society, advanced elegantly and reasonably by the English philosopher and essayist.

George Orwell, *Animal Farm* (1946): A parable about the totalitarian temptation embodied in socialism.

Ayn Rand, *Atlas Shrugged* (1957): A fast-paced novel that is also a capitalist manifesto; it celebrates the entrepreneurs who build and make new things.

Aleksandr Solzhenitsyn, *The Gulag Archipelago* (1974): A devastating indictment of Soviet Communism, and a story of one man's spiritual triumph over the gulag.

Thomas Sowell, *Ethnic America* (1981): Just one—because I had to choose one—of Sowell's many books refuting the presumption that discrimination is the main reason why ethnic groups succeed or fail.

Shelby Steele, *The Content of Our Character* (1990): A revealing look at the psychological underpinning of affirmative action and other race-based policies.

Leo Strauss, *Natural Right and History* (1950): One of conservatism's most important philosophers makes an eloquent defense of natural right against the twin currents of relativism and historicism.

Eric Voegelin, *The New Science of Politics* (1952): A learned, sometimes cryptic, account of liberalism as the modern version of an old Christian heresy.

Evelyn Waugh, *Brideshead Revisited* (1944): One of the great novels of the twentieth century makes the argument against the twentieth century.

Richard Weaver, *Ideas Have Consequences* (1948): The Southern Agrarian diagnosis of the ailment of Western civilization—the decline of belief in an abiding moral order.